DOORSTEP
Wilderness
A WILDER SIDE OF DUBLIN

DOORSTEP
Wilderness
A WILDER SIDE OF DUBLIN

PAUL HUGHES

The Collins Press

FIRST PUBLISHED IN 2014 BY
The Collins Press
West Link Park
Doughcloyne
Wilton
Cork

A CIP record for this book is available from the British Library.

ISBN: 978-1-84889-216-3

Map by Design Image

Design and typesetting by The Design Gang
Typeset in Georgia, Formata, Arid
Printed in Dubai by Oriental Press

Contents

Acknowledgements

I would like to thank all of my family and friends for their support during the creation of this book. I'm also grateful to The Collins Press who have shown such an enthusiasm for my photography, and to Peadar Staunton and Sarah Reece for their superb design and editorial skills.

During the years I have spent photographing the wildlife on this stretch of the River Dodder, I was fortunate enough to meet some great people who lived locally or who worked close by. Many of them stopped to chat almost every day and were much-appreciated company on some very cold and wet occasions.

The strong words of support and the positive feedback they gave me for the work that I had published by the media meant a lot more to me than I think they realised. Their words were positive and uplifting and gave me a boost on many a tough day.

Many thanks to all those people.

Discovery

In the spring of 2008, I was in the middle of a photographic project about the mute swan. I had been regularly taking the train out to Bray harbour, where there are dozens of swans living all year round.

One day, as I pulled into Lansdowne Road train station, I noticed a swan on the River Dodder as I looked up towards Ball's Bridge. Instead of continuing on to Bray, I decided to get out and photograph the swan. It turned out that this was one of a pair of swans who were residents on this part of the river, with their territory extending from Irishtown all the way up the

Here, standing opposite the foxes' den, commuters can be seen boarding an evening train at Lansdowne Road station. The Aviva Stadium dominates this urban landscape.

river as far as Donnybrook. They defended this territory well and would aggressively chase away any other swans that landed there.

At first I was not impressed by this stretch of the river – there was a lot of human debris strewn along the banks. I thought to myself that this was no place for wildlife, but I might take some photos of the swans for a few days and then leave.

How wrong I was! While I was down at the river's edge one day, exploring at the back of what was then the Lansdowne Road Stadium, a fox suddenly appeared from the undergrowth about 30 feet away from me – we were separated only by the fast-flowing river. I could see the fox carefully moving around in the undergrowth at the water's edge. A moorhen suddenly flew back from the middle of the river to where the fox was. It

was then that I saw a couple of her chicks floating on the water, close to the edge of the river and in full view of the fox, but just out of reach.

It was 3.30 pm on a sunny spring day, and it was the first time that I had ever seen a fox hunting.

The chicks had been hidden on the water under some overhanging branches, while their mother was foraging for food for them a short distance away. But the fox had spotted the tiny chicks. Suddenly becoming aware of the fox creeping through the undergrowth towards the chicks, the mother raced back to her babies and began clucking loudly at the fox, attempting to manoeuvre her chicks away from the river's edge whilst keeping herself at a safe distance from the predator. One little chick was finding it hard to swim away from the bank, although it was still just out of reach of the fox. But the fox, now right down by the shoreline, kept trying to stretch its body over the water to grab the chick. The moorhen mother became really frantic now and clucked even louder, lunging at the fox by running along the water beating its wings, stopping just short of the fox. Unfortunately, the moorhen mother created little waves as she did this, which pushed the tiny helpless chick even closer to the river's edge. The outstretched fox, using its teeth, swiftly snatched the chick up and out of the water and retreated back into the undergrowth.

Spellbound, I watched the fox reappear again moments later. It had crawled through a thick weave of branches and was now standing in a small clearing at the river's edge with the chick in its mouth. But it had not finished hunting and had its eye on another one of the chicks, several feet away from the river's edge. It put the first crushed and lifeless chick down on the bank and tried to find a way to grab the second chick without getting into the water. It tried to step out on to some large rocks in the river, but eventually gave up, realising that the moorhen and her last chick were now well out of reach. The fox picked up the captured chick between its teeth and trotted off along the riverbank, under the Lansdowne Road railway bridge, and disappeared into the thick vegetation, heading west up the river. I later discovered that this was the resident vixen and she was bringing the chick back to her cubs at their den.

After witnessing such an intense and dramatic scene, I decided there and then to spend more time on this stretch of the Dodder. With no bean bag or tripod, the camera had to be hand-held and, with an unfavourable shutter speed, I just about managed to get a couple of half decent photos of the vixen hunting the moorhen chicks that day. But this was the first of many scenes that I would photograph over the next four years.

I was hooked.

In the bottom left-hand corner of this image, the surviving chick can be seen out on the water, safely out of reach of the vixen.

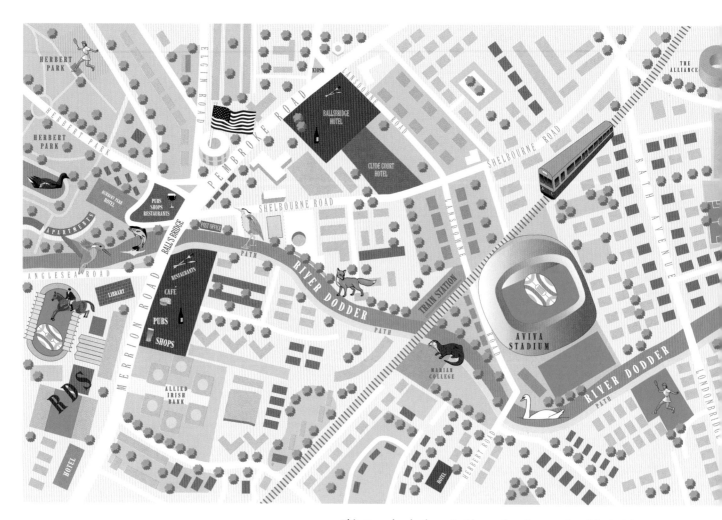

This map clearly shows just how urban the area is – this stretch of the river is surrounded by the human world on all sides.

Doorstep Wilderness is a collection of photographs taken over four years, starting in the spring of 2008 and ending in the summer of 2012. The majority of the photographs were taken on the River Dodder in Dublin, between Ball's Bridge and the railway bridge at Lansdowne Road station. They follow the lives of some of the animals that make their home here, and travel in and out of neighbouring Herbert Park to hunt and visit the pond, and venture upriver to Clonskeagh and downriver to Irishtown – less than a mile away.

On the north side of the river, there is a thin strip of natural riverbank. It is densely populated by a variety of plants and shrubs. Office blocks and apartments stand behind and run parallel to this. On the opposite side of the river there is the old river wall and a pedestrian footpath running alongside, from New Bridge (or Herbert's Bridge), past the railway bridge, as far as Ball's Bridge, with apartment blocks and houses overlooking the river from this side. Every day hundreds of people use this footpath to commute to and from their homes and workplaces.

The sounds of the city are everywhere. Car horns can be heard over the steady hum of traffic passing over Ball's Bridge. Trains can be heard pulling in and out of Lansdowne Road station, and the incessant noise of ringing phones and people's voices are never far away. Despite all this, the sound of the flowing river and its chattering birds manages to break through the cacophony of man-made sounds.

I have always had a love and respect for wildlife. Over the years, I came to the realisation that to observe and enjoy wildlife in Ireland, I usually didn't have to go far from home. The closeness and convenience of our city parks, rivers, canals and coastlines have shown me that great wildlife experiences can be had almost every day. Despite the numbers who traverse the footpath daily along this stretch of the Dodder, most commuters remain unaware of both the extent and the magnificence of the wildlife that lives alongside and in the river down here. Understandably it is easy to assume that a river flowing through a busy urban landscape like this would not be an excellent place to observe and enjoy wildlife, but it is – and you don't need to be an expert to benefit from all it has to offer.

Doorstep Wilderness takes a look at that natural world behind the urban exterior, and explores the circle of life as it plays out between the wild creatures that reside alongside the humans in Ballsbridge, Dublin 4.

The River

The River Dodder is quite clean, considering that it flows right through the city and some heavily populated areas. A wide variety of insects and aquatic creatures provide food for many of the birds and mammals that live on the river. The exotic and spectacularly coloured kingfisher can be seen almost every day. Zooming up and down the river, it hunts the smaller fish, leaving the plate-sized fish for the grey heron and the otter. The river's banks support trees and vegetation that are food and home to birds, insects and mammals, including the fox, the

The view east from Ball's Bridge. This is where many of the events described in this book have taken place.

A view from the pedestrian bridge that crosses the river adjacent to the railway station, showing what a charming and magical place this stretch of the river is. The heavily wooded landscape continues all the way to London Bridge at Irishtown. It was here, just below the bridge and to the left, that I first photographed the vixen hunting the moorhen chicks. This landscape has recently been transformed to build flood-defence walls, so the Aviva Stadium on the left, once hidden by trees, can now be seen.

This well-worn path follows the river down to the railway bridge, continuing on as far as New Bridge (or Herbert's Bridge). The foxes' den is located on the riverbank behind the last tree. Apartment blocks overlook this stretch of the river on both sides.

otter, the badger and small rodents. The swans and other waterfowl feed from the vegetation that the river and riverbanks provide.

The spirit and character of this wild place, in the middle of such a densely populated urban area, is truly realised in the spring and deep into the summer months. The abundance of food and the long hot days give rise to a host of animal activities and truly magical scenes of beauty in a landscape that can, at times, feel as though it's tucked away in a valley somewhere deep in the countryside.

The river here is rarely devoid of the presence of people but, every now and then, and especially at sunrise and dusk, the place is quiet, apart from the sounds of the birds singing and the water flowing. On long hot summer evenings, people sit on their balconies in the apartments that overlook the river, sipping on a beer or a glass of wine, or completely engrossed in a book. Dog walkers and joggers traverse the river's footpath. The stillness is only interrupted by the trains pulling in and out of the Lansdowne Road station, the splashes of fish leaping out of the water in pursuit of hatching flies and the lone peaceful angler slowly wading through the water, gracefully casting their fly-fishing rods.

Bait-cast fishing is common here along the river wall, from Ball's Bridge to the Lansdowne Road railway bridge, from sunrise to sunset, seven days a week throughout the fishing season – from St Patrick's Day (17 March) to 30 September. Men, women and children, of all ages, can be seen carefully placing their fishing rods up against the river wall, having cast their line into the river, patiently waiting for a fish to bite. Quiet laughter and banter is maintained, for they are careful not to scare away a weary fish that just might be ready to take their bait. When a fish eventually does bite down on a baited hook, the fishing line goes tight and is slightly tugged by the fish. This is when the excitement really begins, as the lucky angler tries to reel in the surprised and struggling fish before it can escape from the hook. It is always very dramatic, with the bigger fish putting up the toughest fights and often succeeding in breaking free from the hook. After the fish have been unhooked, held and talked about, and sometimes photographed with their proud captor, they are carefully released back into the river to avoid any permanent harm.

The peace is properly broken, and this place transforms into a great hive of activity, when the Aviva Stadium or the RDS (Royal Dublin Society) hosts a soccer or rugby match or puts

This stretch of the Dodder is a favourite spot for many anglers. Throughout the season they can be seen bait-cast fishing from the wall or, as seen here, slowly wading through the water completely engrossed in the art of fly fishing.

on a concert showcasing some of the world's top musical acts. Thousands of people descend on Ballsbridge and Lansdowne Road and the river's footpath is packed full of people making their way to the events. It is a carnival-like atmosphere with so many there simply to have a good time – all the pubs are packed to overflowing with crowds of people standing and drinking outside the pub doors, the smells from the hot-dog and burger stands fill the air, and shouting and hollering can be heard everywhere, from the cries of the merchants trying to sell souvenirs to the excited yells of the fans and revellers.

In the early afternoons, Monday to Friday, gangs of people working in the offices that surround this area stroll along the river's footpath during their lunch breaks. As to be expected, the warm sunny days bring out the best in people and there is a lot of laughter to be heard. Some stop and talk to the people fishing, who are more than willing to talk about the size and estimated weight of the fish caught that day. At times like this, the activities of the river's wildlife, especially the young foxes, can provide great entertainment for those taking a break from the office, with the cubs playing and foraging along the riverbank. One beautiful hot sunny afternoon, I counted twenty-seven ecstatic people transfixed by the otter as it chased

and caught fish in the Dodder's shallows, less than 20 feet from the river wall and the gathered crowd. Surprisingly, the normally elusive otter was unusually fearless and confident that afternoon, and spent almost an hour in full view of anyone using the footpath.

After lunch, traffic on the footpath is lighter, with only the people fishing and the locals coming and going but, later in the evening, it will be packed with people making their way to the train station and heading home from work. They will be back in the morning, when once again the footpath will be full of people making their way to work.

During the years I spent observing the wildlife here, I met and talked to all kinds of people, male and female, from all walks of life, and of every age. I found it fascinating to note how many things that occurred in the lives of these people were mirrored in events on the river – the search for a partner, then a place to live and have babies, competition for space and territory, finding ways to stay warm in the winter and cool in the summer, and looking for food and a clean and plentiful supply of water for both drinking and bathing.

Autumn

Autumn – the air is cool and refreshing, the beautiful transformation from summer to winter has begun.

Autumn's fruits and nuts provide food for many of the river's inhabitants. A lone fruiting apple tree tucked away on the riverbank has been found and plundered by a variety of birds and foraging creatures. The riverbank's brambles are now full of succulent blackberries, easy pickings for both the wildlife and the people passing by. Conkers can be heard bouncing on the ground as they fall from the towering horse chestnut trees. The riverbank and footpath are littered with colourful autumn leaves.

Once again the heavy autumn rains cause the water levels to rise, making conditions ideal for one of the Dodder's great annual events.

There are many magic moments on the river, but a snatched glimpse of the exotically coloured kingfisher never fails to dazzle me. This rare and enchanting bird reminds me of just how precious and wonderful our waterways are.

The Run

The Dodder's increased water levels are ideal for the returning salmon and sea trout. Both man-made obstacles and natural obstructions are now easier to traverse. Rocks and boulders have been submerged and the fish simply swim past them. Even steeper waterfalls further upriver, caused by weirs or rock formations, are no match for the incredible athletic abilities of the salmon and sea trout. In a spectacular display, they leap several feet out of the water in an effort to gain ground, going up and through the cascading waterfalls. Not all leaps are successful and several attempts are made before the fish overcome these challenging barriers to reach their final destination – the spawning grounds.

Sea trout and salmon are usually seen returning to the river in the summer months, with the sea trout sometimes spotted even as early as April. They continue to return right into autumn. The fish are known then as 'fresh-run' and their skin is silvery in appearance. With more time spent in the river, their skin becomes darker.

Sea trout are, in fact, brown trout that have left the river for the sea. One reason for this is lack of food in the river and a noticeable difference that can be seen in the returning trout is that they are larger, having had access to a greater and richer source of food found in the sea.

This salmon is more than 2 feet in length. It is having quite a battle trying to get up and through the powerful cascade.

Leaps such as this are spectacular to watch and it's hard to believe that this can happen on a city river. This sea trout is still quite silvery, showing that it has just arrived from the sea. Salmon and sea trout have many similarities because they belong to the same family of fish known as Salmonidae – the salmon, however, are much larger than the sea trout and also have fewer spots.

The Journey Home

Salmon and sea trout both return to the river that they were born in to propagate. Both species are protected and cannot be taken from the river. Their numbers are small, but are steadily increasing due to this protection.

In these images, both the salmon and the sea trout can be seen leaping over the same boulders and water cascades in order to reach their spawning grounds.

Both these fish enter the Dodder from the Irish Sea at Ringsend. Their journey takes them past the Aviva Stadium, up through Ballsbridge until they meet the waterfall at Beaver Row in Donnybrook, eventually passing the falls and reaching the spawning grounds.

Not all leaps are successful and the fish hit the rocks more often than not.

This very large fish fails to scale these rocks, having made several attempts already. It will find a better route, preferably where there is a greater volume of water pouring over the rocks. You can see that this fish has been living in fresh water for quite a while as it has no silver on its scales.

Transformations

Sea trout and salmon breeding usually takes place in October or November. By this time the bodies of both the males and the females have lost their silvery appearance, from increased time spent in the river. Their breeding colours also appear and the male's snout is now much larger; they also develop a kype in the lower jaw, a hook turned in towards the fish's eyes, which they sometimes use when fighting male rivals.

Male sea trout are now almost indistinguishable from the river's resident brown trout except for the fact that they are much larger – sea trout can weigh as much as 33 lb. Female sea trout will also mate with the brown trout.

Brackish Water

This stretch of the river is tidal. There are two high tides every twenty-four hours – the waters begin to recede a couple of hours after they first push upriver.

During the high tide, the water level rises and the lower riverbank is now submerged. The sea water, coming up from the Irish Sea, reaches almost as far as Ball's Bridge, only stopping about 200 feet down from the bridge. The salty sea water mixes with the salt-free river water and this mix is known as brackish water. Fish like flounder thrive here and, during the summer months, dozens of mullets can be observed coming upriver on the tides to feed (none of the local anglers is quite sure why they do this – it's a common point for debate) then leaving again with the receding water – they go no further than the brackish water.

Rarely, but every now and again, common seals come upriver with the tides, travelling a couple of hundred feet west of the foxes' den but no more. When they visit, they feverishly hunt the river's fish and terrorise the waterfowl who quickly get of the water before becoming the seals' next meal. The seals also retreat with the receding tide.

Osmoregulation is a process salmon and sea trout have mastered that enables them to live in both the salty sea water and the salt-free river water. This stretch of the river is ideal for the fish – because the water is brackish, it helps the fish adjust slowly to the less saline river water. The salmon and the sea trout hang around here for several weeks.

During their time here, they like to stay hidden in the shadows made by the overhanging branches along the riverbank. Once they have adjusted to the brackish water and then the salt-free river water, they begin to move further upriver towards their spawning grounds.

Fish returning to the sea, or young fish heading out to sea for the first time, will also use the brackish water in this stretch of the river, to adjust to the sea water that lies ahead.

An otter has caught a flounder in the shallows about 200 feet down from Ball's Bridge. This is about as far as the incoming tidal water reaches.

Kingfishers catch fish in their beaks, more often than not, but every now and again they use their sharp beaks to spear their prey. Here, a kingfisher has speared a flatfish, but it soon realises that it can't get the fish into its belly without dropping it. The kingfisher stubbornly sat with the flatfish stuck on its beak until the fish wriggled free and escaped back into the water.

The Otter Family

I could hear a continual high-pitched squeal coming from the river. At first I thought it was a gull or a fox but, to my surprise, it was a young otter. Then I realised that the noise was actually two distinct high-pitched squeals and that there was more than one – a young otter had somehow managed to become separated from its mother and her other two pups.

The otters I see on the river are very active for short periods during the day – they are constantly swimming and diving while their mother fishes for their next meal. They can be seen doing this for up to an hour each time, once in the morning and again in the afternoon. When they stop, they find shelter and remain hidden for several hours in the thick vegetation on the riverbank. At dusk, with the light fading, they all reappear and from then on they are active all night.

An otter pup cries out repeatedly for its mother. It has fallen far behind its family and has become quite distressed. It stops at the river's edge, about 70 feet west of the Lansdowne Road railway bridge, which crosses over the river.

The otter pup's cries are very loud and high-pitched, just like the kingfisher's whistle, and carry right the way down the river. Its mother, seen here, has realised now that one of her pups has fallen behind and she begins to respond to her pup. The two of them call back and forth and, by doing this, the mother discovers the location of the pup.

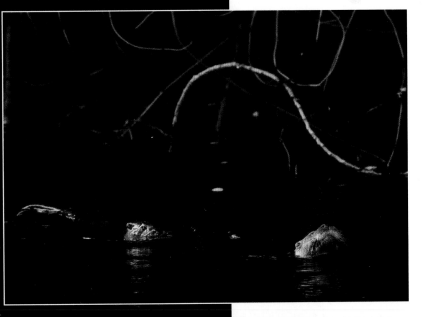

The otter mother doubles back and collects her delighted youngster. Their calls can easily be heard over the constant sound of the flowing water and the hum of the city traffic. The pup swims back with its mother to rejoin its siblings.

Fish caught by the mother otter are given to her three pups. The family move swiftly along the river, the mother continuing to sound out her location and the pups responding. They stop briefly for the pups to take the fish up on the bank, where they spend several minutes eating their meal. Their mother, seen here in the foreground, is about twice the size of her pups. I am not sure how old the pups are, but it is usually two to three months before they are brought out from their underground riverbank home, known as a holt, and taken into the water. Their mother will care for them for fourteen to sixteen months before they have to fend for themselves.

A Place to Call Home

The stretch of the river that this book concentrates on starts at Lansdowne Road railway bridge and finishes at Ball's Bridge, less than a quarter of a mile away. This tree-lined section runs up as far as the old river wall on the north side of the river. The trees include willow, poplar, chestnut, beech and spruce, to name but a few.

The old walls on both sides of the river are covered with moss and lichens, and some plants manage to survive in the wall's cracks and crevices – they hang beautifully over the river. Wall creepers are everywhere and provide greenery throughout the year. They wrap themselves around tree trunks and tree limbs.

The riverbank and its vegetation thin out as they reach the old river wall, a couple of hundred feet east of Ball's Bridge. This is the start of the resident foxes' territory and they can be seen most often between here and the railway bridge, although their territory extends down to the next bridge, known as New Bridge or Herbert's Bridge.

The resident heron spends most of its inactive day standing on a small piece of concrete bank, below and on the east side of Ball's Bridge. This stretch of the river is also his territory and he defends it well.

This beautiful male sparrow hawk finds the river's shallows to be an ideal place to clean its feathers.

A common sight – having spent a considerable amount of time swimming and chasing fish in the water, the cormorant regularly splays its feathers like this in order to dry them out.

The vixen scratches away an itch by the old river wall on the north side of the river, which forms one of the boundaries of her territory. She looks splendid in her thick winter coat.

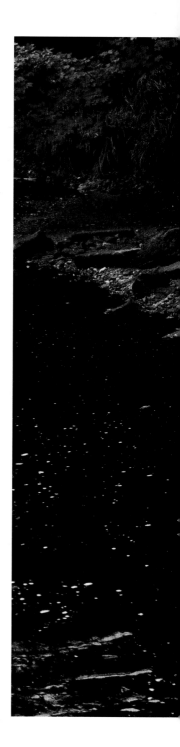

These mute swans are at the centre of this stretch of the river, heading towards the railway bridge. They don't stay long; they are just passing through.

Follow the line of the fallen tree up on to the bank – this is the location of the foxes' den. The incredible forces generated by the river in full flood brought down this once magnificent tree. Almost every year the river changes the tree line. Even the strongest and tallest trees are not safe from the River Dodder in full flood.

The Rat Catcher

Autumn's cold bite has now taken hold and the grasses and weeds that grow along the riverbank have receded or disappeared entirely. Hunting for rodents is easier for the heron, now that there is less vegetation to conceal the small foraging creatures.

The heron spots a mature brown rat scurrying along the riverbank and swiftly grabs it in its beak. The shocked rat squeals and screeches before a short-lived attempt to escape the heron's grip. Within three minutes, having been dipped in and out of the water several times, the rat is swallowed whole and, as always, headfirst.

When it can, the heron dips creatures that are not wet, in and out of the water, before they are swallowed. Without the aid of water, the heron has a longer and more difficult time trying to swallow its prey. The prey is not always dead before it is swallowed.

Many researchers believe that birds are in fact the descendants of theropod dinosaurs that evolved during the Mesozoic Era. The evidence for this theory continues to get stronger. The grey heron reminds me of both the tyrannosaurus rex and the velociraptor. It's an exceptional hunter and a ferocious predator, and always makes me think of prehistoric times. Its charisma and splendour really ignite my imagination and curiosity.

The grey heron is a permanent resident on this stretch of the river and finds its prey both in the river and on its banks. This magnificent bird hunts and eats almost anything it can fit down its long neck. No aquatic creature, small bird or mammal is safe from this patient predator.

The dipper likes to feed off invertebrates such as the nymphs (or larvae) of the river's flies. They can often be seen upturning small rocks under the water and repeatedly diving beneath the flowing water to retrieve small insect larvae. In the bottom photograph, the dipper has broken open the protective casing of a fly larva by bashing it against a rock.

This beautiful male wood duck has just arrived on this stretch of river. It's not a native Irish duck but has been brought here from North America. It has been hunted in the past for its meat and its feathers were used to decorate ladies' hats – this caused a serious decline in the species' numbers. It was a real surprise to see one arrive on the Dodder and spend some time on the river, constantly pecking and chasing the resident waterfowl. The female mallard, seen behind, will certainly be pecked if she gets too close.

Winter

December 2010 – heavy snowfall transforms the landscape. The harsh reality of winter on the river reinforces for me the meaning of the word wilderness. Winter not only alters the familiar landscape but also changes the appearance of some of the river's creatures.

A jackdaw prods and picks at the white blanket that has covered the landscape. This could well be its first experience of snow.

The sound of busy buzzing bees is now long gone. Last summer's hive sits on the icy ground, having fallen from the highest branch of a chestnut tree.

Snowfall marks the beginning of a very cold winter. But the resident heron is hardy and will survive this spell of bad weather. Herons are known to live for up to twenty-five years.

The new scar on the vixen's nose will help me identify her through the coming months. Her fur has thickened all over, keeping her well insulated against the winter chill. Although known as the red fox, her coat has quite a lot of ginger and gold running through it.

The Vixen Marks Her Den

The foxes now become more active during the day. Autumn and winter sightings of foxes along the riverbank are usually far less frequent than in the spring and summer months, when they can be seen regularly throughout the day, busily foraging and hunting for themselves and their offspring. But now that the ground is blanketed with snow, the foxes are out and about looking for food more often than usual.

In winter you may not always see foxes, but you can always hear them – communication between the vixen and the dog fox intensifies, and their eerie barking and vocalisations can be heard day and night.

The vixen has been sniffing around the main entrance of the den that she used last year to raise her cubs. She urinates outside the den and then again about 15 feet from it. She has restaked her claim to this subterranean nursery. This will become home to two litters of cubs in the coming springs of 2011 and 2012.

The den is always vacated by the foxes when the summer is over. Since then, the otter family have occupied it for short periods of time as they made their way up and down the river in search of food – the den was a convenient place for the mother and her pups to rest between journeys. But it will be permanently occupied by the fox family through the spring and summer months.

The dog fox has found the vixen and sightings of the two together are more common. It is now the fox breeding season.

Having spent some time around the den's main entrance, the vixen then urinates at the entrance before leaving – this is known as scent marking.

Unexpected Visitors

The stunning Mandarin duck appeared on the river in the middle of autumn. I counted twelve ducks, more males than females. The male is the more colourful of the two. These ducks are originally from Asia and were brought to Britain in the middle of the eighteenth century as pets.

Some birds managed to escape or were deliberately released. They have been breeding in Britain ever since, where there are an estimated 3,500 breeding pairs. A few have found their way to Ireland and there are reports coming in that they have begun to breed here. A couple of pairs have remained on this stretch of the Dodder, but I have yet to see them breed or produce any young here.

Three Mandarin ducks – two male and one female – make their way up the river, passing the RDS (Royal Dublin Society) that lies adjacent to this stretch of the river.

A colourful male Mandarin duck does its best to find something to eat beneath the snow.

Survival of the Fittest

Moving through the thick snow and fighting the cold is energy sapping. Finding the next meal is now more important than ever.

The deep snow is slowing the dog fox down. Sometimes the foxes find it difficult to move through it. The rough weather lingers on.

Grey squirrels (not a native Irish species) are very active on this stretch of the river and can be seen daily, foraging between the branches and on the ground along the riverbank. They do not hibernate in the winter but are much less active than during the warmer months. Their thick winter coats will help them get through the cold days ahead.

Spring

The river is full of new sights and sounds brought by the spring. Soon the air will be filled with the sound of chirping chicks begging for a meal from their parents. Slowly, the bleak winter landscape is being transformed and optimism abounds – the animals bet on a food surplus and begin to propagate their species.

These young fox cubs love to show their affection for their mother by jumping on top of her. Their exuberance never fails to lift my spirits. They always appear to be full of energy and life, and have a natural curiosity, a playfulness, a boundless enthusiasm, that is a joy to watch. Having observed the fox family's daily displays of affection and tenderness, I find it easy to empathise with them.

The Heron's Toughest Prey

The grey heron catches eels regularly on this stretch of the river. These eels can be over 3 feet in length and as thick as a baseball bat.

Fighting to the end, the heron never has it easy with this most slippery of prey. The eel's muscular snake-like body often wraps itself around the heron's beak. These confrontations can be lengthy and bloody. It's rare to see a heron draw blood with its prey but, unfortunately for the eels, the heron has no choice but to throw the eel to the ground and then stab it with its beak, until it has been disabled enough to be swallowed whole and without a fight. Sometimes, however, even this is not enough, and the eel wriggles back up and out of the heron's throat and the violent stabbing starts again.

The European eel is an endangered species and is protected by law. It is an extraordinary creature and can live up to thirty years.

The heron is having a bit of a job trying
to unravel this eel from its beak.

The eel twists and turns as it tries to break free from the heron's tight grip.

The eel is thrown to the ground and stabbed repeatedly by the heron. It's not long before the eel is defeated and easier to control – then the exhausted eel is swallowed whole.

The egret shows up every now and
again on this stretch of the river
and is sure to attract the attention
of anyone passing by as well as the
resident wildlife – it is hardly
inconspicuous.

City River

The riverbank is strewn with city debris deposited by
the heavy flooding and careless littering by some of
the people passing by – an eyesore in contrast to the
beautiful wildlife that lives here.

Suddenly a stunning little egret alights on the
bank, between the foxes' den and the railway bridge.
This bird is not a native Irish bird but arrived from
Europe and started breeding here in 1997. It eats fish,
frogs and other aquatic creatures, and also snails and
insects. However, I have only ever seen it catch and
eat small fish on this stretch of the river.

Washed up on the bank, a gift from the river, this
foot-long brown trout will make a great meal.
The first to arrive is a little robin, who can be seen
daily, foraging around the river's edge, but it turns
out that this meat-eater is not too fond of fish. The
robin moves on and so do I, but when I return a
couple of hours later, the fish's remains are gone.
How it died and who ate it remain a mystery.

Heavy rain lasting several days can unexpectedly flood the best-built nest and destroy all its eggs.

Rain and Flooding

The swans dedicate time to looking for a suitable place to build a nest that is safe from flooding.

Finding the right spot on the river is not always easy, however, and, on one visit, I saw that the swans had already spent several days building their nest only to realise that a small rise in the water level, from a not-so-heavy downpour, had submerged it. They eventually found a safer spot much further up the river and successfully laid and hatched all their eggs.

This male mute swan, known as the cob, desperately tries to grasp an egg that has floated out of the nest. Sadly, the eggs will be lost to the rise in the water level and they will have to wait another year before they can try again.

Here the cob carefully settles himself down on the nest. He is relieving the female, who has sat on the nest incubating the eggs for several hours. They will alternate their duties like this repeatedly throughout the coming days. The black flesh on the cob's beak swells during the breeding season, distinguishing it from the female.

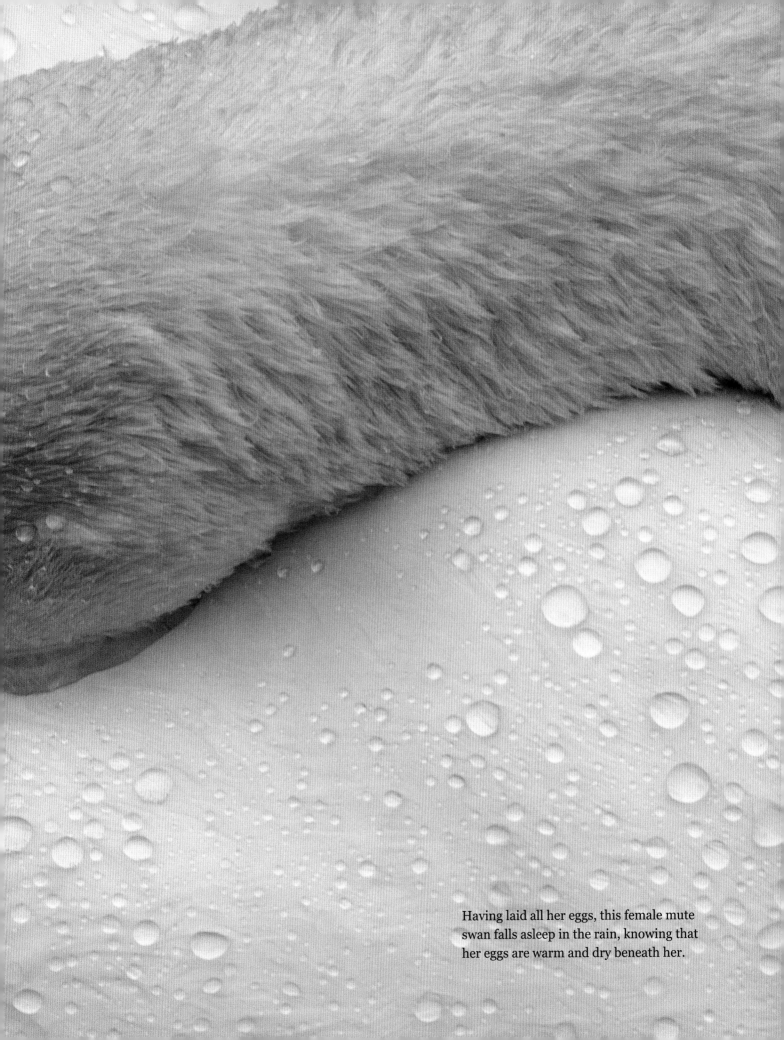

Having laid all her eggs, this female mute swan falls asleep in the rain, knowing that her eggs are warm and dry beneath her.

Subterranean Nursery

Foxes are born blind and deaf. They are born below ground, in their parents' den, also known as the earth. The vixen stays with the cubs, keeping them warm and fed, for their first couple of weeks. During this time, the male fox takes care of the vixen and regularly returns with food for her.

The cubs here are usually born in the middle of March and start to appear above ground at the beginning of April. By this stage, the vixen has already left them alone, but returns regularly throughout the day with fresh meat in the form of dead birds and rodents. Along with this solid food, she nurses them with her milk at regular intervals several times a day.

The foxes excavate a hole just wide enough to enter and exit the den quickly.

I had seen the vixen coming and going close to the den but, until I saw a cub, I could not be sure that she had successfully given birth to a new litter. Then, one afternoon, this infant climbed up and out of the den. It only surfaced for a few minutes, before wisely disappearing back down into its hidden subterranean home.

The broad-leaved plants that surround the foxes' den are known as winter heliotrope. This evergreen plant flowers in the winter months, producing a beautiful lilac-pink flower. It provides great cover for the young foxes, keeping them hidden while they scurry around, and the cubs, or kits, like to play with the dried leaves and twigs that fall to the ground from the trees above.

Winter heliotrope was originally introduced from north-west Europe and is now widespread. Similar in appearance to our native butterbur, it grows all along this stretch of the river and indeed covers almost all of the River Dodder's banks.

Distractions

At this time of year, the drakes are eager to mate with female mallards, even those taking care of their newly hatched chicks. So the females with hatchlings find themselves continually fending off the drakes, while opportunistic hunters like the heron and the lesser black-backed gull recognise this as an opportunity to catch one of the chicks while their mother is distracted.

The drakes clamp down hard with their beaks on the females' head when they are mating. They pull on the head feathers trying to get a grip while they mount the hens. Injuries caused by drakes can often be seen on the females' heads. Accidental drownings even occur, especially when several drakes attempt to mount a hen at the same time – unable to breathe, the submerged female loses her life.

This drake is intent on mating with this female mallard, even though she has already got a large brood of newly hatched ducklings. Drakes eager to mate with the hens continuously harass the mothers with their chicks. Trying to escape from the relentless pursuit of the males usually results in the ducklings being left alone and unprotected from potential predators. On this occasion, the female succeeds in chasing the drake away, causing quite a splash.

Here to Hunt

The lesser black-backed gull is adept at creating panic and disorientation amongst a young duck family.

From its vantage point above the pond in Herbert Park, where it is circling repeatedly, the gull spots the vulnerable and defenceless hatchlings. Depending on their mother for protection against this fast-moving predator, they react instinctively when they see the large bird above their heads with its big, sharp beak – it's as if they know that this particular bird is a predator and that their lives are in danger.

Their mother calls out frantically, summoning her chicks to her side for protection. But the experienced gull knows exactly how to scatter the young chicks as the mothers' panic increases. Its speed is impressive as it swoops down on the chicks that dive quickly below the water for cover. Swooping in and out above the duck family is a very effective and safe tactic for the gull – the ducklings can pop up anywhere and usually appear several feet away from their mother. The experienced gull knows this and spots a duckling popping up some distance from its protector. It swiftly snatches the duckling from the surface of the water, then lands on the footpath next to the pond. Within seconds the tiny chick is swallowed alive and whole.

A newly hatched brood of up to thirteen ducklings can be wiped out before sunset by such ruthlessly efficient predators. Sometimes, with her brood gone, the mother cries out, heartwrenchingly, all day long for her chicks to return.

This lesser black-backed gull has caught a male mallard duckling. The lesser black-backed gull is 20 to 26 inches in size and has a wingspan of between 4 and 5 feet – an ominous presence for a tiny duckling.

The ducklings flee as the gull approaches. Many of them escape into the foliage and water, but unfortunately not all. These ducklings were left alone and unprotected – their mother had flown to the far side of the pond to escape the relentless attention of the eager drakes. This gull had been watching the drake's behaviour towards the chicks' mother and knew from experience that, at some point, the ducklings would be left alone and unprotected. Its patience paid off and it managed to snatch and eat two ducklings before their mother came back, having being chased some distance away by the persistent drakes. The mother returned oblivious to the fact that two of her chicks were gone. I have seen this particular gull watch for, and take advantage of, opportunities like this many times.

This crow is very vigilant, keeping a watchful eye over the activities on the river and the comings and goings of the vixen nearby.

The Hooded Crow

The hooded crow is a very clever bird. I have watched the crows find shellfish down on the coastline – they have ingeniously found a way to crack open the tough shells and consume the contents. One lucky crow managed to find a large mussel and, not being able to break its hard shell with its beak, it flew 50 feet above the rocks and dropped the shellfish repeatedly down on to the rocks, until the shell shattered. The crow then easily ate the contents of the shell.

This stretch of the river has a pair of hooded crows and what a couple of characters they are! They have recently taken up residence on the river, arriving sometime in 2011. Since then, they have harassed and bullied just about every creature, including the foxes.

The grey squirrels certainly don't get any peace – the crows chase them through the tree canopy. The squirrels leap from branch to branch trying to avoid the crows' sharp beaks. They are swift and agile, but the hooded crows manage to get in a few sharp pecks to the squirrels' tails and hindquarters. The crows do not tolerate the squirrels' presence in the tree tops, possibly for territorial reasons or out of fear of having their nest plundered and their offspring preyed upon – grey squirrels are known to eat bird eggs and young chicks.

The crows watch everything and always seem to be the first on the scene when anything edible washes up on the riverbank – they are a strong presence on the river.

Another duckling predator, the opportunistic hooded crow spies a baby duck that has fallen behind and lost sight of its mother and siblings.

A New Family

The vixen has given birth to six cubs this year. Last year, she gave birth to five and, with the help of the dog fox, they successfully raised them all. Soon the baby foxes will be seen scurrying in and around the riverbank's vegetation, biting and tasting almost everything they come across.

The vixen is careful not to be noticed as she returns to the den, where her vulnerable young reside. She communicates with her cubs very quietly, signalling her approach using soft vocals, similar to that of a whimpering dog. She uses the same sound to call down into the den, summoning her cubs to the surface. The cubs are always pleased and excited when their mother returns. They come scurrying up and out of the den to greet her. Once they have finished feeding, the cubs like to stretch their legs and can be seen playfully running and hopping through the vegetation that surrounds them.

The young cubs are sometimes transfixed by the new sights and sounds that each day brings. They have an intense but cautious curiosity and can be seen many times dashing out of fear back down into their subterranean lair. The loud cracking calls from the heron are enough to get their little legs running.

The cubs' charcoal-coloured fur is already beginning to brown. From brown it will turn golden and eventually ginger. Their blue eyes will also change, becoming a golden yellow as the weeks pass.

The vixen hears something in the branches and lifts her head to sniff the air. She can often be seen with her large ears pricked, sniffing the air repeatedly, trying to locate and identify potential prey. All kinds of birds and rodents can be found hiding in the plants on the riverbank.

The vixen has returned to feed her six hungry cubs. The cubs squeeze in and under their mother and latch on to one of her teats. Several minutes go by before the vixen is satisfied that all six cubs are well fed – depending on how hungry they are, the cubs can spend anywhere from two to ten minutes suckling.

Along with providing regular meals throughout the day, the vixen also grooms and cleans the cubs. Spending so much time underground, their woolly coats are bound to get dirty and probably attract a lot of fleas and other insects. Using her tongue and teeth, the vixen spends several minutes on each cub, licking them and nibbling them from top to bottom.

There is never a dull moment on the river – there's always something to watch. And situated at the top of the bank, the cubs' den gives them a great view of the water below, as well as of the myriad people who walk, run and cycle along the footpath on the opposite side of the river.

The otter is back – it's been many weeks since its last visit. The otter will hang around on this stretch of the river for several days then, as always, move on up or down the river. It will be another few weeks before I will see it again. I wonder if the fox cubs saw it while it was here; it does a lot of fishing close to the den. Here the otter is finishing off a fish it has caught in the shallows. The waterfowl keep a watchful eye on the hunting otter from a distance – they also make up part of the otter's diet.

This female chaffinch has found something edible
by picking in the sandy soil. Unfortunately, the
riverbank is also littered with human debris.

Days of Plenty

At this time of year, insects are crawling all over the ground, and seeds from the surrounding vegetation, both on and off the river, are blown or fall on to the riverbank.

The birds and fox cubs can be seen foraging daily, picking in the soil for some of its insect dwellers. Many of the birds can also be seen nibbling on the seeds strewn along the riverbank.

This robin is seen here beneath the foliage lining the route that the vixen and dog fox use regularly to traverse the riverbank when the tide is out.

Unlike the male, the female blackbird is brown in colour.

A pair of beautiful goldfinch have established residence on this stretch of the river, but have not yet produced any offspring. Hopefully they will soon. This bird is collecting what appears to be nest-lining material.

Natural Instinct

One of the fox cubs spots a moorhen sitting on a branch overhanging the river. The tide is in and the moorhen is protected by the surrounding water. Just like its mother, the cub will not get into the water. Although they can swim, the foxes down here never attack the waterfowl while they are on the water. But the cub thinks it can get down to the bird by walking along the fallen tree limb that leads directly to the moorhen. Nervously it puts one foot forward ... but that is all. It is not brave enough to walk along the log that hangs over the deep water.

By now, the moorhen has spotted the cub and begins to cluck loudly in the cub's direction, but it never leaves its perch and continues to preen its feathers, while the frustrated cub looks on.

The cub had a real desire to get at the moorhen – it was surprising to see it in hunting mode at such an early age. But its mother had brought back many birds for her young to eat, so it was probably not surprising that the cub had both an appetite for birds and the instinct to hunt them.

The cub decides not to walk along the
dangerously placed fallen tree limb.
The moorhen keeps an eye on the young
cub, but never moves from its perch.

Twilight on the Riverbank

Although the foxes are active throughout the day, darkness finds them at their most active. The streets are emptied of people and have now become their domain. Food dropped or dumped by midnight drinkers are easy pickings for the urban fox.

With the light fading and night approaching, the ducks and all the river's waterfowl will have to find a safe place to lay their heads. Many of the ducks gather on a dry rocky beach close to Ball's Bridge. It is probably the safest spot on this stretch of the river. The riverbank is fraught with danger, especially now that the vixen has many mouths to feed. Her increased hunting activity lessens the chance of a duck surviving a night on the bank.

A female mallard carcass has been brought back to the cubs and dropped off outside the den. Either the dog or the vixen caught it that night or just before dawn – it was there when I arrived just after sunrise.

Almost always, after catching a good-sized fish, the otter will swim back to the bank and eat its meal. Here, it has just finished eating its catch and is about to re-enter the water and start fishing again. It is getting dark and this otter will be active right through the night.

Night is close. A wood pigeon has landed at the river's edge for a sip of water – it's rare to see one on the ground after dark. This beautiful bird makes probably the most relaxing and calming bird song I have ever heard, often creating the impression that the river is a tranquil place. But there are many meat-eaters here and not a whole lot of peace.

When night arrives, bats can be seen darting around the streetlamps positioned alongside the river. Flying insects attracted to the lights are rapidly caught by these speedy mammals. There have been three species of bat identified on this stretch of the river – Leisler's bat, the soprano pipistrelle and the common pipistrelle.

Day and night, the vixen hunts and forages for her hungry young family. Pigeons, both feral and wood, are never safe from this experienced hunter.

Just like all the birds that wash themselves at the river's edge, this female bullfinch is constantly looking up and around for any predators that might have spotted her in this very vulnerable position. Sparrow hawks and foxes are never too far away. Her noisy splashing can attract unwanted attention, so the bird needs to be ready to get up into the air quickly and out of harm's way.

A mallard drake takes a cautious sip down at the water's edge. The foxes' den is only 20 feet behind him.

Always near dusk, and after a long day hunting and foraging for her family, the vixen stops at the river's edge for a well-deserved drink, before heading off once again into the night to hunt and forage. As she approaches, all the small birds and waterfowl quickly vacate the riverbank.

Heightened Senses

Birds that forage on the ground, such as the blackbird, are ideal prey for the fox.

Blackbirds root around under the bramble thickets along the riverbank and the fox can be seen doing the same thing. The fox's eyesight has adapted to enable a hunting fox to move quickly and safely through thick, sharp, protruding vegetation. Its sharp vision and reflexes allow it to avoid being poked in the face and eyes by brambles and shoots, particularly useful when chasing smaller prey, such as rodents. For a bird that has rambled deep into the undergrowth, a quick exit when under attack might not be possible. I have seen foxes with blackbirds in their mouths more than any other bird.

The vixen stands in front of the den with the remains of a young magpie in her mouth. She has been making her usual soft whimpering vocalisations, waiting for her young to exit the den and retrieve the dead bird. The cubs sometimes hang around the lower entrance to the den and it is here that she will feed them her catch.

The City's Gift

The Aviva Stadium at Lansdowne Road is just minutes away from the foxes' den. After a big match or music concert, the streets are filled with the leftovers of the thousands of people that filled the stadium. Half-eaten hotdogs and meat-filled sandwiches are dropped or discarded – the vixen takes full advantage of this bounty to fill her cubs' bellies.

The vixen has no favourites and the cubs have no concept of sharing – as usual, they fight for the best portions of the food brought back to them. Here, the over-excited cubs pull apart the carcass before racing off to eat their piece of the prey. The vixen leaves them to get on with it.

The vixen drops a half-eaten sandwich outside the den. She will continue to collect and bring back hotdogs and bread rolls while they are available.

Home Improvements

The den is now in need of expansion, possibly because the cubs are getting bigger and more active every day, or it could be for extra ventilation. The entrances act as escape holes from predators too – whatever the reason, the vixen gets to work.

Currently, there are two entrances to the den – one at the top of the bank and one just below. The vixen spends several days excavating a new entrance that will link up the existing chambers and connect both the top and the side entrance. Her activities have not gone unnoticed by her cubs and they watch with great curiosity as their mother excavates around their home.

When she's finished, the young cubs enjoy exploring their newly renovated home and make good use of the new entrance. They are even closer to the river now and can enjoy front-row seats to all of the day's activities – the grey heron regularly hunts for fish just below the freshly dug entrance. Venturing down to the river for a drink of water exposes the very young foxes to everything that might have an interest in them – good or bad. They are still quite nervous and can be seen scampering back into their hole at any sudden sounds, especially those made by the hooded crow. Large birds of prey are known to hunt young foxes and even the adults. But the new entrance provides them with quick access to the hidden chambers of their den.

Using her paws, the vixen tunnels into the side of the bank and shovels out the soil from the new entrance to the den.

A cub pops its little head out from the den and has a look around
for the noisy bird that frightened it. The cubs almost always sniff
the air as soon as they reach the surface.

Trout of this size are often caught by the heron. The heron fishes this spot regularly and in full view of the cubs sitting outside the den. Its feathers almost seem to be mimicking a cloudy sky. For any prey looking up from the water, I suspect that the motionless heron blends in well with the backdrop of the sky, effectively making it difficult to spot.

There are at least a dozen gorgeous long-tailed tits living in the trees above the foxes' den. They can be seen together zigzagging between the branches as they forage for and catch small insects.

Sun Worshippers

The fox is a great lover of the sun and can be spotted during the day lying in a favourite spot, soaking up the sun's rays.

With the advent of spring, the heat from the sun has increased and the young cubs quickly work up a thirst dashing around in their woolly coats. The convenience of having a fresh supply of cool and clean drinking water on your doorstep is not wasted by this fox family.

The cub's coats are becoming more golden every day. The strong sunlight in this photograph highlights the change.

The young cub has caught up with one of its siblings and decides to have a drink from the river too. With the temperature rising, the young cubs can be seen regularly coming down to the river's edge to drink from the cool fresh water.

This song thrush better watch out – thirsty young fox cubs are on their way down to drink at the river's edge.

This greedy cub runs as fast as it can with the remains of a pigeon in its mouth – its siblings are in hot pursuit. When the other cubs finally catch up, a big fight breaks out, lasting several minutes. The cubs' high-pitched cries and screams are once again heard up and down the river. Their mother had buried the pigeon a good distance from the den this time. Her clever cubs have been trained well, however, and it did not take this youngster too long to locate today's feast.

Time to Learn

The vixen has begun to bury the cubs' food under the ground, several feet from the den.

When she's finished her task, the vixen heads off once again to find more food for herself and the cubs.

The cubs, who are now venturing outside the den without their mother being there to protect them, immediately begin to sniff the air as they exit the den. One lucky cub picks up the scent and excitedly runs around with its nose to the ground, quickly locating the hidden food.

This, I am sure, was the vixen's way of teaching the cubs how to find food for themselves and also encouraging them to explore their surroundings, but at a safe distance from home. The vixen continued to do this daily, hiding the food further and further from the den as the cubs got older.

As dusk approaches, the little cubs are bounding with nocturnal energy. They playfully jump and pounce on one another.

Mother Duck to the Rescue

The thunder and lightning had ended, the rain had stopped and it was a beautiful evening.

Danger was circling in the skies above, however, lapping the pond in Herbert Park from one end to the other over and over again – a lesser black-backed gull was looking for a lone duckling.

Ducklings often become separated from their mothers and siblings, and their mothers are constantly quacking to them, reminding them to stay close. Lesser black-backed gulls will attack and grab a duckling from its mother's side but, in so doing, risk injury from the mother duck trying to protect her young. This technique also takes a lot of time and energy and they cannot always get past the defending mother.

Today the lesser black-backed gull has landed on the pond and, using its paddle-shaped feet, it begins to patrol the pond slowly and quietly. Almost immediately it spots a duckling that has strayed several feet from its mother's side. The prowling gull cautiously watches the mother for any signs that she might be aware of its presence and intentions as it gets ready to snatch the duckling.

The mother duck has not spotted the gull but the duckling has, and begins to chirp loudly, looking for help from its mother. Sensing its window of opportunity might be running out, the gull takes to the air and chases the now terrified and fleeing duckling. Unable to escape the faster predator, the duckling dives under the water and swims away, a technique commonly used by the ducklings – they often can escape this way, popping up 10 to 15 feet away, back by their mother's side. But not this time. The gull is too quick and catches the diving duckling.

By now all the ducks on the pond have spotted the gull and an outburst of hysterical quacking erupts everywhere. The duckling's mother charges in, startling the lesser black-backed gull so much that it drops the duckling. The gull is now on the run itself, fleeing to get out of harm's way. The duckling escapes unharmed, but its concerned mother immediately checks it for injuries. On another occasion, I saw a mother successfully fend off a heron, the lucky chick falling from the heron's beak. But one of the duckling's legs was damaged and it could not paddle, so the mother quickly beat her offspring to death using her beak. Was she putting it out of its misery? Or will a lame duckling attract unwanted attention from predators?

The mother duck swoops in, in a desperate attempt to save her chick. The duckling drops from the startled gull's beak.

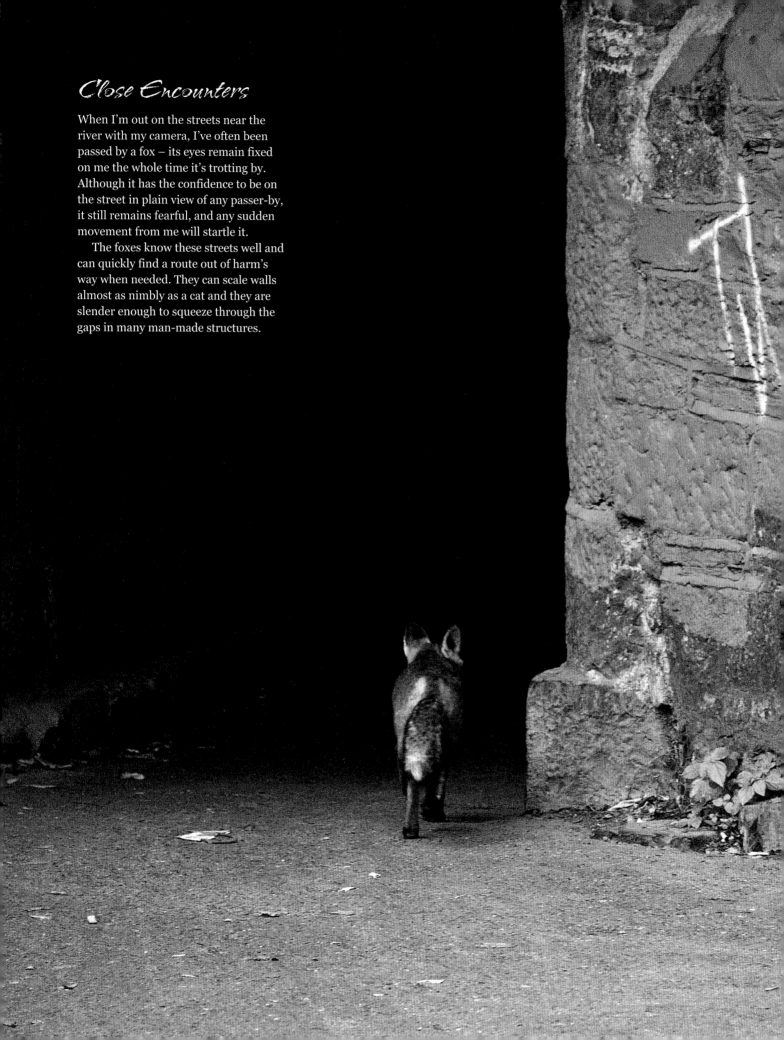

Close Encounters

When I'm out on the streets near the river with my camera, I've often been passed by a fox – its eyes remain fixed on me the whole time it's trotting by. Although it has the confidence to be on the street in plain view of any passer-by, it still remains fearful, and any sudden movement from me will startle it.

The foxes know these streets well and can quickly find a route out of harm's way when needed. They can scale walls almost as nimbly as a cat and they are slender enough to squeeze through the gaps in many man-made structures.

Seeing a wild animal like a fox on a city street in daylight hours is always thrilling.

Foxes are very nimble and almost cat-like in their ability to scale man-made barriers. They confidently walk along thin walls and, when they cross the railway line, they quickly trot along the even thinner steel rails without faltering.

City traffic takes its toll. This young fox was killed by a vehicle on Pembroke Road, Ballsbridge, in front of the American Embassy. During the years I spent photographing this area, I saw three dead foxes, all killed by vehicles.

The mother helps this tiny cygnet find its way out by upending
the egg, using gravity to help the hatchling inside drop out.

New Life Emerging

The male and female swans both take turns incubating the eggs, routinely switching places throughout the day. The female rarely leaves the nest for the last few days before the cygnets hatch out and the male never strays far from her side – he attacks any creature that comes anywhere near the nest.

Brown rats make daily attempts to get close enough to the nest to steal and roll away as many of the eggs as they can. The rats, however, have no chance of stealing an egg from this pair, who snap aggressively at all the rats that get too close. Previously, I have seen a lone rat roll away an unhatched and abandoned swan egg without too much effort but, despite all the rat's work and effort, after a short fight a bigger and more aggressive rat took the egg away.

The swans do a great job and eight out of their nine eggs hatch – in the end the rats manage to get one unhatched egg after all.

The swans' nest was built on the riverbank, next to the pedestrian footpath that runs the length of this stretch of the river, from the railway bridge down to New Bridge (or Herbert's Bridge). During the weeks that the swans had been incubating their eggs, many people who used the footpath to commute took a great interest in their wellbeing. As a result, many people were present as the eggs hatched, watching from the footpath. It was, for us all, a fascinating event to witness, and we all felt very privileged.

The swan eggs are about the size of an average chocolate Easter egg.

The cygnet has arrived. Its siblings will soon follow.

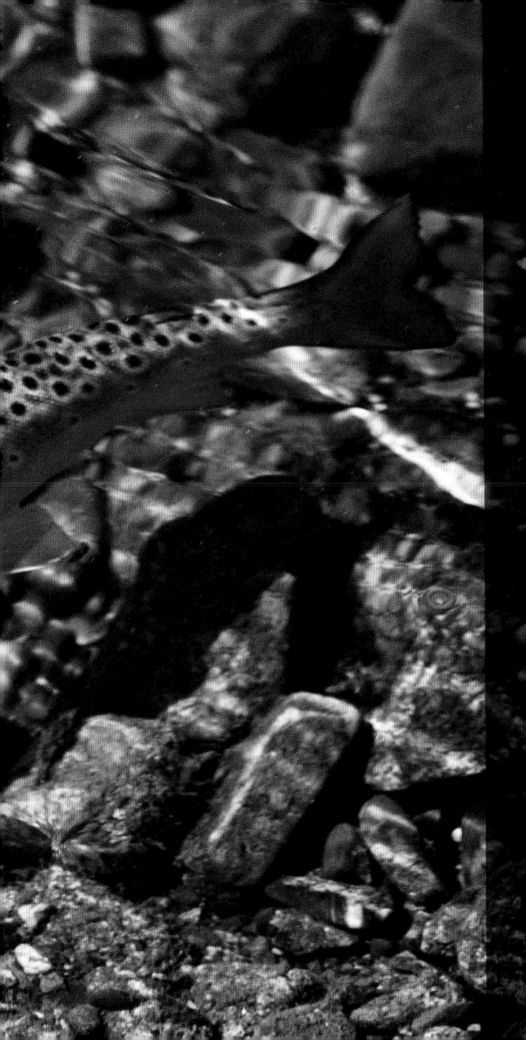

Nature's Gift

Thousands of hatched flies hang over the river like smoke rising from a campfire.

The flies lie beneath the rocks on the river bed as larvae, waiting for the right water temperature to trigger a mass hatching and the exodus from their shells. Fish take advantage of this and catch and eat as many flies as they can, during the flies' journey from the river bed, up and out of the water and into the air.

On this stretch of the river, you can spot trout patiently waiting for hatching flies to rise from the river bed. They can be seen snapping away, catching and eating the flies as they float up to the surface. Some flies are simply plucked from the water's surface as they float around the hungry fish.

This brown trout lies in wait for a fly. It snatches at almost everything that comes its way.

Both wagtail chicks cry out when they see the beak full of flies. One of the chicks will be left out this time but the wagtail parent returns rapidly with food for the second youngster. The swarm of flies is enormous – there are plenty of flies to be caught easily and swiftly.

A Feast for the Wagtails

The wagtail parents target these vast clouds of zigzagging flies. Using their excellent flying skills, the wagtails pause and hover like hummingbirds, repeatedly snapping amongst the flies until their beaks are full, before returning to and feeding their constantly hungry chicks spread out along the river's banks.

Many lifeless flies can be seen floating on the water's surface, with some washing up on the bank. The wagtail parents pick up these flies from the water's edge, then simply walk back to their hungry chicks waiting right behind them on the riverbank. Without their parents' help, and using their own initiative, the chicks also begin to find and eat the flies.

Flies can be seen up and down the Dodder and are a food source for many birds and fish. This wagtail has almost filled its beak but will catch a few more flies before finding and feeding one of its chicks. Swallows and swifts can also be seen flying high and low, harvesting the huge swarms of flies that congregate close to Ball's Bridge.

The wagtails do not rely solely on the flies and feed a wide variety of insects to their chicks.

Feeding Frenzy

Having only just developed the ability to fly, five very young wagtails still depend on their parents to feed them. Positioned in different spots along the riverbank, they wait impatiently for their beaks to be filled.

The wagtail chicks all chirp loudly, hoping to be noticed and fed first by their parents. Between them, the parents manage to find all the chicks and almost all their offspring are fed equally.

The parents work at a furious pace, collecting insects and feeding the chicks all day long – they display an amazing amount of energy and the chicks never have to wait too long for another insect delivery. This relentless feeding lasts for five to seven days, by which time the chicks' flight feathers are fully formed and they are left to fend for themselves.

The five vulnerable wagtail chicks managed to avoid being attacked and caught by any of the river's predators. What with all the noise they generated trying to get their parents' attention and sitting on the ground for long periods of time, I was absolutely amazed they had never been pounced upon by the vixen, especially on the first couple of days that they were fed outside the nest. The chicks were very slow to react to the ducks and the moorhens who wanted to take a closer look at the noisy newcomers, and I felt that, if the foxes had taken a closer look, the young wagtails would have been easily caught.

The chicks, with their limited flying abilities, try to follow their parents, but end up having to land, unable to keep up with their parents' high-speed flying. The chicks consequently find themselves spread out all along the riverbank. But their cries are so loud that their parents do not find it hard to locate them. At last, another meal is delivered to this hungry chick.

This wagtail chick waits to be fed again by its parents. Its four siblings have also found a spot to perch and they too wait for another insect meal.

This wagtail parent displays its phenomenal hovering skills, feeding its chick with care while still in flight.

Silence

In contrast to the noisy, frenzied feeding of the wagtail chicks, the swan family emanate a sense of tranquility as they paddle up and down the river, quietly foraging for food.

Unlike the wagtail chicks, only capable of limited flight but enough to escape most predators, the cygnets are flightless and very vulnerable. It serves them well to be quiet and keep a low profile on the river, to avoid attracting unwanted attention, especially when they forage on the riverbank or leave the water to rest.

Nine eggs hatched eight cygnets this year. They are proudly ferried up and down the river as their parents search for food to feed their large family. The female swan likes to have her newborns safely tucked away on her back. In this way, she has no difficulty transporting all eight cygnets along the river when they are too tired to paddle alongside.

The cygnets and their mother calmly make their way through the water, foraging and playing as they go.

Welcome Opportunities

Both the vixen and the dog fox regularly and quietly sneak through the undergrowth here in search of prey and, in this very spot, on my first visit to this area, the vixen easily snatched the moorhen chick that was too close to the riverbank. The cygnets are always very vulnerable to attack when they are on or close to the bank – and this stretch of the river, between the Lansdowne Road railway bridge and New Bridge (or Herbert's Bridge), is where the dog fox takes short naps during the day. It is best not to wake the sleeping dog fox.

A fox will wake up immediately at the sound of any kind of noisy activity around the river, whether it be ducks fighting or an animal in distress, especially the frantic chirping of a baby duck or cygnet that has fallen behind its mother and siblings as they paddle up and down the river. I have observed both the vixen and dog fox rapidly awaken from their slumber and, with their ears pricked, hone in on the direction of the sounds and, more often than not, investigate the possibility of catching an easy meal.

The dog fox has not stopped helping out its family and it will be back soon with food for the cubs. Somehow he has managed to lose his tail but seems to be coping well without it, although he still has a problem with his eye that developed sometime during the winter months.

The dog fox has found a good-sized sandwich that will please the little cubs.

Dappled shadows over carpet moss. Nose to the ground, the cubs like to sniff as they walk along the riverbank.

Flying insects always get the attention of the young cubs, bees and butterflies in particular. They will leap and swipe at the buzzing bee and the hovering butterfly. However, they are not very successful at catching them and the insects can easily avoid the cubs' attack.

Resting, but not quite asleep – a spot 20 feet from a foxes' den is always fraught with danger.

Hot Bright Days

Winter is now long gone. You can feel the stretch in the days. The sun rises earlier and sets later. Energy levels are up and energy sources are plentiful – food is no longer scarce.

Biting tails and instigating fights are popular pastimes for the cubs.

Food from the River

Many food items get washed down the river and settle on the banks. Any animal that scavenges as part of its quest for food will be amply rewarded every now and then.

The fox cubs are now confident enough to wander about the riverbank in search of food for themselves in between the meals that their parents bring to them. Although they have overcome some of their earlier fears, they still will not forage too far from the den – just near enough so that they can make it back and down into the den within a minute or two, if necessary.

Today two cubs hit the jackpot and find the remains of a very large salmon on the riverbank. The hot late spring sun bakes the discarded carcass; the stench of rotting fish is hard to miss. The cubs are visibly excited by the enormous meal they have found.

Even with a feast this big, the concept of sharing is unknown to the growing cubs and, as usual, a fight begins. One cub tries to escape, running off with all the carcass for itself, but is quickly pursued by its sibling and a tug of war ensues. The sounds of the excited, battling cubs can be heard all along this stretch of river. All the squabbling gets the attention of the other cubs and they come racing out of the den – now four are fighting for the best portions.

After several minutes of this they all manage to get a sizeable piece of the fish's remains and dash away separately to eat their feast in peace.

The cubs enjoy one another's company while they forage and explore their surroundings, but the first one to find food does its best to keep the meal all to itself and not-so-friendly altercations always ensue. Here the cubs are pulling and dragging a salmon carcass over the riverbank. They are barking and yelping like young dogs, while they hop and jump around, trying to create enough leverage to rip the carcass apart.

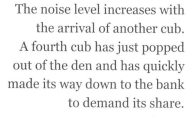

The noise level increases with the arrival of another cub. A fourth cub has just popped out of the den and has quickly made its way down to the bank to demand its share.

The cubs explore deep into the riverbank's vegetation. They are now more familiar with, and less afraid of, their environment.

The Battle for Mating Rights

For several days now, the male moorhens have been fighting one another on and off throughout the day.

Using mainly their legs and feet, they beat down hard on each others' heads and bodies. At times they become so aggressive that killing seems to be their aim, although there are no actual fatalities. The fighting males' loud vocals do not go unnoticed and at one point they narrowly miss being caught unawares by the vixen.

Eventually there is a victor – the female's original mate successfully defends his rights to mate with her.

On one occasion, I watched a pair of these moorhens fight. The stronger of the two kept the weaker one under the water as long as it could before it eventually broke free and escaped, while the challenger took off, running down the side of the riverbank. I am in no doubt that the stronger moorhen was trying to kill its opponent by drowning it.

The moorhen uses its feet to beat down rapidly and repeatedly on its opponent's chest.

The battle continues on land. The moorhens are violent and appear to be trying to inflict serious damage. Their fighting technique reminds me of a rooster fight. I would not be surprised to see one of these fights resulting in the death of one of the duellists.

Disputes and fights are common among all the
river's birdlife, not just the moorhens. Here, a
thirsty male chaffinch drops down to the river's
edge to quench its thirst. A resident bluetit notices
the newcomer and drops down for a closer look –
it goes unnoticed by the drinking chaffinch.

Not happy with this new bird, the smaller bluetit went
on the attack and chased the chaffinch away.

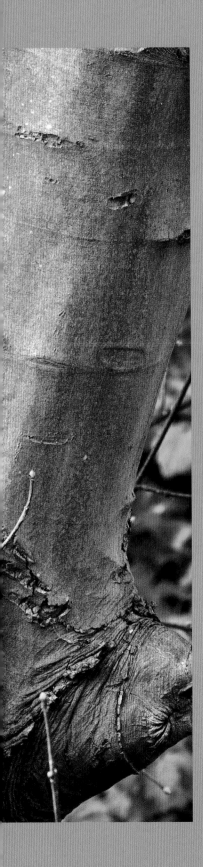

Summer

It is now June. The arrival of summer has transformed this stretch of the river into a lush green haven, full of vibrant colour provided by the river's flowering plants. The landscape is throbbing with life – animal activity has increased, especially among the birds who are busying themselves collecting material to build their nests.

Other birds, whose nests are already full of hungry hatchlings, are constantly on the move, flying here and there in search of food for their hungry broods that hatched out in the spring.

The grey squirrel responds to the increasing temperature and sheds its thick winter coat.

A picture of serenity – the calm before the storm.

A Perilous Journey

The cygnets' parents take their young up and down the river in search of suitable vegetation for them to eat. They do this every day, then return to the nest to bed down for the night. The cygnets spend their nights wrapped warmly under their mother's wings. Their experienced parents know the river well and are aware of its many dangers. Unfortunately, however, an unforeseen threat to the survival of their offspring lies ahead.

Nearing the end of the cygnets' first week of life, their parents decide to venture further down the river in search of food. The swan family have to go over a fast-flowing man-made weir to reach their destination. On their return, making their way back up the river to the nest after a long day of foraging, it's clear that climbing up the weir would have dire consequences for the young family – it has become an impassable barrier for the tiny cygnets.

Desperately, their parents try every route around the weir and even make attempts at carrying the cygnets on their backs to get them over the weir, but to no avail. The swan family couldn't make it back to the safety of the nest site and had to sleep on the gravelled river bank.

Two days of continuous rain later, the river's water level rose dangerously high for the swan family and the cygnets were swept away while their parents were taking an afternoon nap. The adult swans woke suddenly to the chirping of the distressed chicks and frantically tried to collect their young, who did not have the strength to swim against the powerful torrent. All the cygnets, except for three, were lost to the river.

One of the survivors, drenched and exhausted, dragged itself onto the riverbank, but a magpie had been watching and quickly attacked. The cygnet tried to escape but the magpie kept up the attack and the cygnet died minutes later. The bird ate only a small amount of the chick and discarded the rest. Another cygnet, lodged between some overhanging branches at the river's edge, was rescued by a young man who waded into the shallows. He carefully put the cygnet into a shopping bag and, using a rope, lowered the youngster down from Ball's Bridge onto a small patch of bank below – the cygnet hopped out and made its way back to its parents and sibling. The next day, only one cygnet remained – the swans tried again to get over the weir, but with no success.

A few days earlier, a cygnet had become trapped in the rocks under Ball's Bridge. Its parents did not appear to know how to get it out, so the cygnet remained stuck, chirping away all the rest of that day and into the night.
It was alive and still chirping when I arrived early the following morning. Its parents were still at its side – finally I saw the male reach down and pull the cygnet out using its beak. But what looked like a happy ending was actually the opposite – minutes later, the male beat the youngster to death with its beak. The chick did look exhausted and its legs appeared to be injured, so I can only assume that its father was putting it out of its misery.

By the end of that week, even the sole remaining cygnet was nowhere to be seen – all the swans' offspring were now lost to the power of the river and its predators.

One of many failed attempts to get the cygnets past the weir. All five cygnets fall from their mother's back.

In a display of extraordinarily uncharacteristic behaviour, the male mute swan allows the only surviving chick to ride on its back as it tries to overcome the weir. After many failed attempts he too is forced to give up.

The three cygnets are washed downriver.

The tiny cygnet trapped in the rocks under Ball's Bridge.

When the female is ready to mate, she stops and bows her head and waits for the male to mount her. During the course of the day, the male is at her side, encouraging her to mate again. When he has successfully impregnated her, this courtship stops.

Mating Moorhens

The victorious male moorhen locates the female and they mate. They will do this several times throughout the day and will later find a suitable place to build their nest.

After mating, the male displays himself in this way every time – bending forward and fanning his feathers. He then struts around in front of the female, posturing for several seconds.

Summer Coats

Both the resident foxes and the squirrels adapt to
the changing seasons. Shedding their winter coats,
which keep them warm in the colder months,
they prepare for the hot days ahead, when their
summer coats will help keep them cool.

The vixen has begun to shed her thick
winter coat. A large patch of hair has been
shed from her back already. All red foxes,
both male and female, do this.

Urban Backdrop

Under the guidance of the vixen, the cubs are introduced to the human world that surrounds them. She does not take them out onto the streets, but in and around the apartment complexes and office buildings built near the river.

The vixen often takes the cubs out and about but never too far from the den. She seems to be encouraging them to explore the landscape more and more by themselves now.

This cub is standing on the wall built on part of the upper riverbank. The wall runs along about two-thirds of this stretch of the Dodder and acts as a flood defence for the office buildings beyond. It's a pedestrian area and a lifebuoy hangs from a post just behind the cub.

The cubs display total trust and admiration for their mother.

The Spring Heron

Straight from the nest, this new arrival looks prehistoric; more like an Australian emu than a heron. Its shaggy and half-formed feathers indicate that this bird was born and raised in this year's spring, although not on this stretch of the river. It clearly has not yet developed its hunting skills fully and often misses in its attempts at nabbing fish, where an older, more experienced bird would not.

A pair of hooded crows that arrived here last year have been terrorising and bullying every other creature on the river, especially the resident heron, who was dive-bombed, pecked at and persecuted relentlessly until it learnt to stay out of the crows' newly established territory. The hooded crows have no trouble chasing this nervous bird out of their patch on the riverbank either.

The crow sneaks up on the young heron and bites its tail feathers. The young heron lets out a loud screech from fright and surprise.

Ebb and Flow

Low tide, when the lower banks are revealed, is the most active time on this stretch of the river. The water here is clear and shallow, ideal for the heron who likes to walk through the water as it hunts for the river's aquatic inhabitants.

Both small birds and the fox family can be seen regularly foraging along the lower banks. The kingfisher has more success catching fish in the shallow waters at low tide, although it can and does catch fish when the tide is in.

The swans forage below the water for aquatic plants. They will also eat some of the vegetation growing along the bank and floating on the surface of the river.

One day I met a retired butcher who had with him a bag of uncooked rashers and sausages. To my surprise, he began handfeeding the swans – they ate up the bag's contents in no time. The man said he had been feeding rashers and sausages to the swans on Dublin's Royal Canal for years.

It's fascinating to watch all the different creatures on this stretch of the Dodder making use of their environment – utilising the multitude of elements, from rock and soil, to leaves and bark, and everything in-between, to provide food and shelter and places to build nurseries to raise their young.

Spending time here is never boring – the river is an incredibly dynamic and beautiful place. For me, every animal living on or passing through this stretch of the river has some unique and extraordinary quality that makes it impossible to pick a favourite. I find that observing any of the river's inhabitants closely will always reveal something that enthralls me.

For me, scenes like this reveal the magic and charm that make this stretch of the river such a wonderful place.

The adult mute swan's neck feathers become saturated from being submerged beneath the water in search of food. The swan frequently shakes out the water with quick twists and turns of its neck.

The dunnock can often be seen hopping around the riverbank, finding insects and seeds here and there. It keeps itself busy, picking up small insects that crawl over the moss-covered rocks.

Time to cool off – this herring gull makes use of the river's clean water to wash its feathers.

The black-headed gull is certainly the nosiest on the river. Groups of these birds can be heard chattering and bickering loudly throughout the day.

The lesser black-backed gull has had a lot of practice developing its hunting skills. It is more successful than not at catching the waterfowls' chicks.

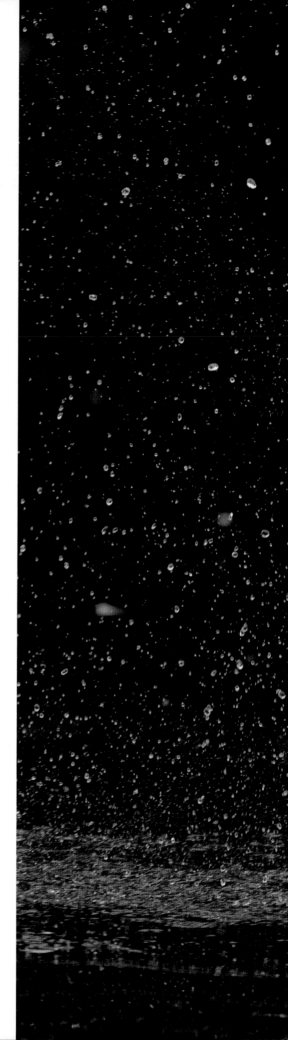

Predators

Killers come in all shapes and sizes, and meat is part of the diet of almost all of the creatures on this stretch of the river. Fish catch flies, birds catch fish and flies, other birds and small mammals. The fox eats all of the above.

The waterfowl, however, are safe as long as they stay in the water, as the foxes have no great love of the water.

The young cubs are now energetic and fearless explorers, and their great curiosity takes them up and down the riverbank, foraging at greater distances and for longer periods of time away from the den. They stay within this stretch of the river, though, between Ball's Bridge and the Lansdowne Road railway bridge.

While drinking, the cub keeps one eye on the waterfowl floating on the river. The cubs' curiosity takes them further and further along the riverbank, on the same routes used by their mother and other fox families before them. Darkness is just minutes away – the sun is setting.

The mallard mother and her chicks have come onto the bank to rest. The lower entrance to the foxes' den is just 10 feet behind her.

Life and Death Decisions

After a morning paddling around in the shallows, the mallard mother and her tired chicks leave the water and find a spot on the bank to rest for a while.

For a duck, and especially one with so many vulnerable young chicks, the riverbank is a very dangerous place to be. Predators that cannot hunt on or avoid the water have now got a greater chance of catching the mother or her young.

Within minutes of them settling on the riverbank, a magpie lands on a branch above their heads and assesses its chances of snatching one of the chicks without being attacked by their protective mother. In the end it decides not to attack and flies off.

Unwisely, however, the mother duck has decided to settle down just below the lower entrance to the foxes' den. And a hungry young cub is about to wake up and venture outside.

The young fox slowly emerges from the den, looking a little bit groggy. But he immediately senses something moving below.

The cub makes a dash for the duck family, only narrowly missing its prey.

Startled, the mother and her terrified young family race back into the river and paddle furiously away from the rapidly pursuing young fox, quacking, splashing and chirping. The panicked chicks continue to dash around on the water until their mother composes herself and they move, more calmly, away from the young fox on the bank.

The young fox can only watch as the mallard family paddle out of reach.

The Vixen's Welcome

The cubs sense when their mother is on her way back to the den and are visibly excited at her arrival.

Magpies cackle loudly when the vixen appears – they watch her closely as she makes her way along the bank. A dozen or more hop from branch to branch and tree to tree, following the vixen back to the den. This happens every time the magpies see the vixen or the dog fox, but not so often when the smaller cubs appear.

Is this an act of caution or fear? Or are they trying to intimidate her, hoping to drive her from what they perceive as their territory along the bank?

It has been two months since the cubs first appeared above ground outside the den. They glow with health and vigour, and can be seen playfully wrestling with one another daily.

The young foxes sprint towards their mother when they sense her imminent arrival, hoping to be the first to get food. Despite their increasing independence, they are still regularly nursed by their mother. Lactation is thought to stop much earlier than this, at about six weeks.

The cubs like to nudge their mother's mouth with their snouts. This cub may be hoping the vixen is carrying food. Sometimes the cubs are simply silently communicating with their mother, greeting her and expressing their affection for her.

A Close Encounter with a Creature of the Night

I am used to hearing the sound of heavy rustling in the bushes on the riverbank; it's usually a fox on the hunt for a small rodent. But on one particular sunny afternoon, the rustling was unusually loud and, for the first time on this stretch of river, I saw a badger.

I was amazed to witness, at such close quarters and in daylight hours, a healthy-looking badger collecting vegetation for bedding to take back to its set. It foraged around for quite a while, then disappeared into the undergrowth. The very next day, at around the same time, it was back again, doing exactly the same thing. Badgers, it seems, get fresh bedding every day.

This time the fox cubs were up at this end of the riverbank; the badger's chosen area was only about 700 feet from the den. Two of the cubs were playing and foraging right next to the badger, who was hidden from sight – only the noise and the swaying of the bushes indicated its presence. One of the cubs quickly noticed the heavy rustling in the bushes and went to investigate.

Seconds later the cub came racing out of the bushes, yelping loudly. It was unharmed but it did not stop running until it was over 100 feet away. The badger, on the other hand, at about twice the cub's size, was not at all bothered and continued to collect bedding right into the night.

When darkness descends, the nocturnal badger becomes very active along the riverbank. This environment has plenty of places for it to dig for worms, and there are numerous rodents and nesting birds for it to hunt. The badger will spend the night hunting and foraging under the cover of darkness.

The badger is collecting dried foliage from the riverbank to serve as bedding in its subterranean home. It rolls the gathered material of dried leaves and grass into a ball and drags it several feet along the bank and back into its underground home. This material will help keep the badger warm and comfortable while it sleeps through the daylight hours.

The railway is used by both the grey squirrels and the foxes as a short cut around the river. The vixen often trots in complete confidence down the platform at Lansdowne Road, in full view of the commuters waiting for the next train to arrive.

The vixen is on her way back to the cubs with a surprise. From time to time she will bring gloves and old shoes to the young foxes. They like to bite and tear into the tough materials, possibly helping with any teething problems they might have. Rubber and leather shoes and gloves are strewn around the foxes' den.

The cubs' foraging is beginning to pay off. The vixen likes to encourage this by continuing to bury portions of food for them within their usual range from the den. The cubs are always on the lookout for an easy meal, however, and will try to steal food from their siblings. Plenty of real and violent fights break out among them this way, and the sound of crying and whimpering cubs can be heard along the river every now and again.

Routines

Without fail, the vixen makes her way down the river, navigating the same well-worn route along the river's edge.

Every fox born on the river over the past few years has used all or at least parts of the trails she and the dog fox use daily. In many places the vegetation has been totally flattened, just to the width the fox needs – these routes are called runs.

These trails lead to exits that take the foxes off the riverbank and into the urban landscape. These exits take the foxes over walls or under wood or wire fencing – the fox scrapes away the soil under the fencing, removing just enough to squeeze through.

All the creatures living on the river have their routines and knowing their routines makes it far easier to study them.

The vixen has left the cubs and is heading off down the riverbank, along the same familiar trail she has been using for years. This part of the bank is regularly used by the otters when they want to rest, but they keep out of sight, hidden by the thick vegetation.

The vixen returns to the den. As usual, she sticks her head into the hole and calls lightly to her young, inviting them to follow her.

On higher ground, this nimble young fox surveys its surroundings.

The sun's rays have just broken through the dark night and a new day is beginning. The young foxes have been out and about all night and, as at dawn every day, they make their way back to the den. They will rest there for a few hours, resurfacing at about nine o'clock. They usually awaken at this time for a drink of water. Then they play around for a bit before either going back into the den or resting on the side of the bank outside the den's main entrance. This is their morning routine.

Harris' Hawk

Early one morning I was in Herbert Park trying to capture the lesser black-backed gull hunting the pond's newly arrived ducklings. My attention was diverted by the sound of a dozen or more black-headed gulls squawking loudly while they circled around and dived at one of the nearby trees. This kind of behaviour usually indicates that a predator of some kind has arrived. So I went over to investigate, expecting to see a heron perched on one of the branches.

Well, I was surprised! The most magnificent bird of prey was sitting high in that tree. This formidable predator was almost 2 feet from tail to crown, and its talons and beak were both large and very sharp. I had never seen a bird of prey in the wild like this before. It appeared too big to be a buzzard and did not resemble the eagles that have been reintroduced into the wilds of Ireland. It also had tassels hanging from its feet. Later, a more experienced bird-watcher studied my photographs and identified the bird as most likely to be a Harris' hawk, originally from the southern United States and South America, which had probably escaped from a falconer.

The bird of prey cast an inquisitive eye at the annoying gulls that circled above its head. It did not show any fear, but decided to move to the tree on the opposite side of the pond.

Several mallards were resting just below the tree. When they spotted the predator above, their reaction was like nothing I had ever heard from them before. The mallards' cries and quaking differ at the approach of a heron or a lesser black-backed gull – there is definitely greater fear in their vocals when they see the heron. The sounds they made on seeing today's threat were distinctly different. There was a real intense sense of fear and anxiety that I had never heard before. They must have known that not only were their ducklings' lives in danger but also their own. It was a chilling moment that caused the hairs on the back of my neck to stand up.

The raptor was found again by the noisy gulls, so it finally left, finding peace and quiet outside the pond, by concealing itself in one of the park's taller, leafier trees.

I have not seen the bird since then, but it was an encounter I will never forget.

On seeing a raptor of this size, I can appreciate
the newborn fox cubs' natural fear of the
predatory birds on their stretch of the river.
A bird of prey the size of a Harris' hawk could
easily catch and kill a young fox cub.

This young sparrow hawk eats a small bird brought to it by its mother. The young hawk has fledged (learnt to fly), but still relies on its mother to hunt and find food. It will be several more weeks before it, along with its two siblings, can fend for itself. An eerie silence descends over the river when the sparrow hawks are hunting – the normally chatty birds become silent in an attempt to conceal their location from this impressive hunter. When the sparrow hawk attacks, it displays incredible flying skills, swiftly weaving its way in and around the twisted and tangled woods along the riverbank in pursuit of its feathered prey. Once caught, the unfortunate bird is taken to a branch or clearing on the ground. Struggling and crying out under the hawk's claws, the bird's feathers are rapidly plucked by the hawk's sharp hooked beak – it is then eaten alive.

One Eye Open

Common amongst all the river's inhabitants is the fear of being attacked. Being alert to all the potential dangers is paramount to their survival. They are all habitually watching and listening and constantly looking over their shoulders as they go about their ways.

A break from this discipline can result in death.

This young cub stays vigilant as it drinks.

Mallards like to upend themselves, or dabble, and stick their heads and necks under the shallow water in search of their favourite food, such as insects, molluscs, crustaceans and aquatic plants. They will also find and eat food that floats on the surface of the water. Taking a break from dabbling on the water, this female mallard stands tall, surveying her surroundings for any potential threats to her life.

The Golden Hour

The river is full of birdsong as the light of day fades.

Sunset, like sunrise, is a beautiful time on the river, with the last, softer rays of sun bringing out the best in nature's creations. For a photographer, the way the light can illuminate the riverbank so perfectly is extremely rewarding – this is known as the Golden Hour or the Magic Hour.

Some birds make their way down to the river's edge for a final sip of water before darkness falls and it gets too dangerous for them to drink.

Wood pigeons are very cautious when they come down for a drink and do not stay on the ground for too long. The last light of the day illuminates this scene.

Fights with other birds, which involve the plucking and biting of feathers, leave their mark. But this magpie is only moulting – it is discarding its old feathers to grow new ones.

The vixen has a quick drink of water before she locates her cubs, who are now spending most of the day above the ground and further away from the den.

The vixen has found one of her cubs down on the riverbank. She still likes to make sure they are clean so, when she finds them, she immediately sets to work grooming their beautiful coats.

The Dog Fox

The dog fox is bulkier than the vixen – his face is wider and more rounded.

Sightings of the dog fox on the river are much rarer than those of the vixen. But he does find food for the cubs and is usually spotted in the early hours of the day, around sunrise, making his way towards the den with something for the cubs to eat.

One day there was a brief amount of frantic noise from some blackbirds up on the riverbank. I could see them diving and darting in and out of the low-hanging tree branches close to the river. Moments later, the dog fox appeared with a male blackbird in its mouth. He took it straight to the den – the cubs came racing up and out, sensing his arrival. The dog fox set the lifeless bird on the ground and two of the cubs fought for the best portions.

Foxes are also known to bring live prey back to their cubs so that the youngsters can practise their hunting and killing skills.

With the loss of his tail and the shedding of his winter coat, you might think, wrongly, that the dog fox was suffering from mange. The dog fox uses the same routes as the vixen. The fuchsia plant seen here is not native to Ireland, but has been introduced from Chile and Argentina.

Landscaped Gardens

The river running through Ballsbridge is surrounded on both sides by office blocks and people's homes. Their landscaped gardens support a wide variety of plants and these attract many insects that contribute to the diet of the river's resident birds.

The foxes can often be seen during the night, foraging around the gardens.

A bumblebee brushes off some excess pollen before buzzing off.

The Vixen's Trepidation

The vixen's favourite route takes her downriver and over the rocks that lie beneath the railway bridge.

Twice every twenty-four hours, however, the tide generated by the Irish Sea pushes its way up the river. The salty water passes the foxes' den and stops just short of Ball's Bridge. The water level rises and the river's bank is concealed for several hours – until the tide recedes the vixen's route along the bank is inaccessible.

I have never seen the vixen enter the water to swim or wade, and even when she has a chance to catch one of the river's waterfowl she will not enter the water. She always behaves nervously when confronted with any water that she has to cross to get to her intended destination.

The vixen's attention is caught by one of the feral pigeons that nest between the steel girders under the railway bridge. She cautiously tests the water's depth and decides that it is just about shallow enough for her to cross.

Still looking very fresh from the nest, the young heron's hunting skills are noticeably improved. The eel struggles to break free.

On the Prowl

The young foxes are becoming more aware of their role as predator.

They are beginning to resemble their parents in behaviour and their predatory actions are becoming more deliberate, hinting at their potential to be the most feared hunter on the riverbank.

The young foxes are gaining in confidence. This cub has picked up a scent by sniffing as it walks along.

A male blackbird bathes dangerously close to the lower entrance to the foxes' den. This is no place to linger.

Moorhen Parents

The moorhens on this stretch of the river usually have five or six chicks, although in general they are known to have up to eight chicks. They are very attentive parents and both the male and the female are involved in raising their chicks.

The moorhens can be seen throughout the day finding food – a varied diet of vegetation and insects – for their chicks. They feed their chicks from beak to beak.

The moorhens like to keep their chicks hidden in the thick vegetation while they are off searching for food for them.

The moorhen chicks are constantly begging for food. The squeaky sounds they make sound like the hinges on an old gate pushed open again and again. They are extremely noisy and easily give away their location, even when hidden.

The Observant Predator

The moorhens in Herbert Park have done well so far and kept their chicks safe and invisible, but one day the heron comes to rest in a tree overlooking the nest on the island in the pond. It spots the parents coming and going with small portions of food for the chicks.

The chicks want food constantly and are continually chirping. The heron hones in on the noisy chicks and suddenly becomes interested in the activity below. Before long, the heron has located the chicks and sticks its long neck down between the thick vegetation. It simply reaches into the nest and snatches one.

A moorhen parent sees what happens and comes racing back, managing to lunge at and beat the heron's beak with its feet, but the heron does not drop the tiny chick. It takes off and lands high in the tree above, quickly swallowing the chick alive.

Meanwhile, the moorhens on the Dodder, between Ball's Bridge and the Lansdowne Road railway bridge, also had to deal with the heron and its aggressive pursuit of their chicks. The heron made many attacks on this pair's chicks, but the moorhens were brave and did their best to defend their family – they managed to keep the remainder of their brood out of reach of the hungry predator under some thick vegetation at the water's edge. The heron could not get at them there and grew tired of the fight the moorhens put up. Eventually it left, and the deafening noise of the clucking moorhens and the screeching heron was no more.

Two days after I took my photographs, however, the three chicks that the moorhens were defending were not seen again.

Down on the Dodder, the moorhens attack with their feet and beat back the huge predator. They are aggressive and brave – the attacking heron could inflict serious injury or even death. They repeatedly attacked the heron and managed to prevent it from stealing any of their young. The heron almost had one of the chicks, but the moorhen's fierce defence left the heron with nothing but a dried leaf in its mouth. The heron gave up and made a hasty retreat; the moorhens calmed down and went back to caring for their chicks.

The grey heron has just snatched the moorhen chick from within the thick vegetation on the island in Herbert Park's pond.

Successful Attacks

The other moorhen family has only one chick left from the original brood. The mother desperately tries to conceal her tiny baby from the heron who has not yet spied the chick. But, eventually, the heron spots a tiny movement behind the mother's wings and, without hesitation, lunges forwards and snatches the chick from the mother's side.

The moorhens haven't been very successful at raising chicks on this stretch of the river. The presence of such unforgiving predators takes its toll and I have only seen one moorhen chick reach maturity over the past three years.

The moorhen mother nervously tries to conceal her chick from the heron's eyes. She has fanned her wings and hides the chick behind them.

Her efforts are in vain – the heron has spotted her only surviving chick and attacks. The moorhen cries out and tries to fend off the huge predator. She rapidly beats the water with her feet and gets ready to lunge at the attacker, but the heron darts swiftly in and out with her chick before she can do anything to stop the attack.

With the chick in its beak, the heron is gone in a flash, avoiding being attacked or damaged by the chick's frantic mother. It stops a safe distance away downriver and, with one gulp, consumes the tiny chick whole and alive, just as it does with a freshly caught fish.

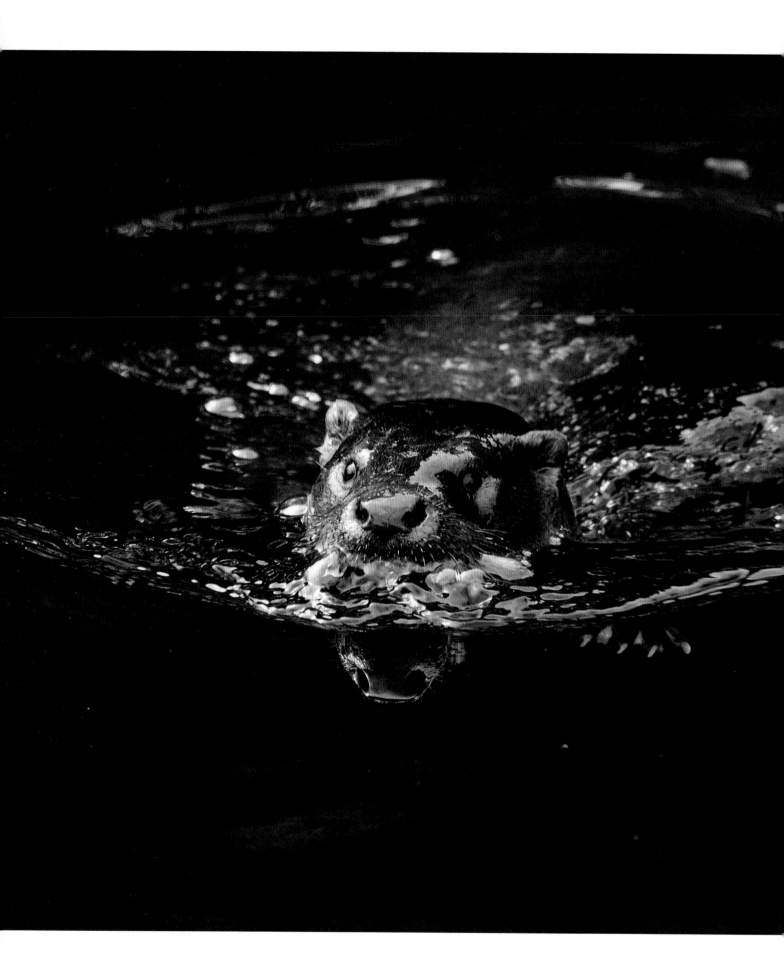

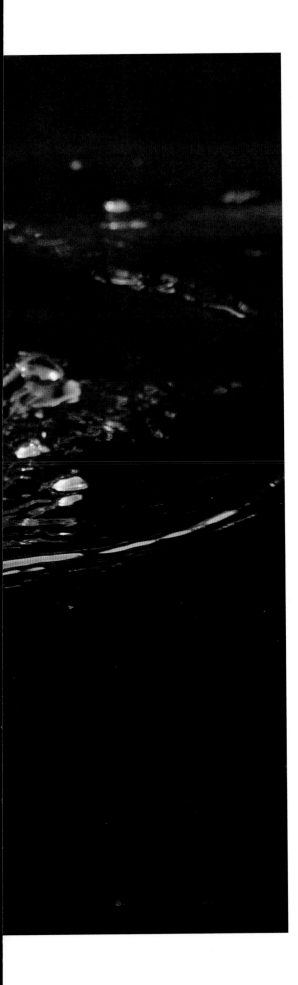

A Graceful Hunter

The otter is a real joy to watch as it effortlessly swims and dives through the Dodder's clear waters.

Master of its domain, it turns over the rocks on the river bed and swiftly snatches any unlucky aquatic creatures residing there.

This otter repeatedly dived beneath the surface and upturned rocks on the river bed in search of prey.

The otter is an elegant and graceful swimmer, swiftly pursuing and catching its underwater prey.

The young foxes rely heavily on their sense of smell to find a meal. This one is sniffing out a favorite prey – the brown rat.

On High Alert

During daylight hours, the young foxes, now almost fully grown, are easily spotted on their way down the riverbank.

Any kind of heavy movement in the vegetation on the bank does not go unnoticed and waterfowl that happen to be out of the water quickly run or fly back to the safety of the water. With their noses to the ground, the young foxes sniff casually around the riverbank and beneath the surrounding plants. Sometimes they venture out of the den alone but often they like to hang around in pairs.

Every now and then the foxes sense an opportunity and chase down a sitting duck or a small bird perched on a low branch. They get surprisingly close to their prey and it's easy to see how a slightly unaware bird, with a lowered guard, could be caught by these youngsters, who are now confident hunters and well adjusted to their environment.

When in true hunting mode, stalking prey amongst the riverbank's vegetation, the foxes tread much more carefully and quietly and are harder to detect by the animals that live here.

Noisy rats reveal their locations.

The constant
prowling up and
down the riverbank
always pays off.

With just two chicks remaining from her
original brood of twelve, this mallard mother
takes her offspring into the dark shadows on
the river's edge, hoping they will be out of
sight of any prowling predators.

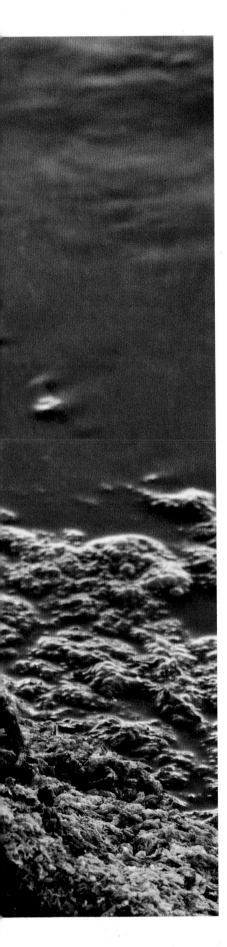

Brown rats are often on the menu for both the foxes and the heron on this stretch of the river.

Just caught. The young fox has taken the young rat down onto the lower bank. The rat's back legs were damaged at the time of capture, but initially it did try to crawl away. It now lies motionless, unable to run away.

Stealth and Speed

The young foxes' hunting skills have developed sufficiently for them to catch brown rats.

This unfortunate brown rat was caught while out and about foraging up on the riverbank. A young fox heard the rustle in the foliage and began to leap and pounce around the spot where the rat was.

The fleeing rat was just not fast enough and was caught and carried down to the river's edge by the swift fox. Then the fox, acting like a cat, began to play with the rat.

The fox first set the rat down and waited for it to attempt to run away. Then the fox leaped and pounced on the rat, repeating this sequence a number of times, sometimes tossing it into the air as well – it appeared to me as if the young fox were practising its hunting and killing skills.

After more than ten minutes, the fox finally ate most of the rat. It buried the remainder but returned later to unearth it and finish it off.

Heavy Losses

Mallards average between eight and thirteen chicks per brood. Sometimes, however, all of the female's brood can be wiped out in a day or two, even before the end of the chicks' first day off the nest, by the numerous predators looking for an easy meal.

But there is always a drake eager to mate again. A female can have a second brood in the season and try once more to get at least some of her chicks to maturity.

This mallard's original brood of thirteen chicks has been reduced to two and one uninvited guest. The tiny tufted duck chick joined the brood a couple of days ago, having drifted from its own mother's side. At first, the mallard pecked at the chick many times but the chick stayed anyway. It had to swim a lot quicker than the larger mallard chicks to keep up so I was amazed that it lasted as long as it did. But, in the end, none of the chicks survived, most likely caught and eaten by the herons or the gull.

The Grey Heron Is Hunting

With a loud shriek of dominance, the heron announces its arrival. Its bloodcurdling shrieks create panic among the waterfowl, whose terrified responses can be heard up and down the pond. The quacking is deafening and intensifies as the heron begins its hunt for flightless and vulnerable ducklings.

Frantic and terrified, the mother ducks' vocals are enough to send the ducklings racing back beside them for protection. But this will not be enough to escape this predator's lethal intentions.

The heron spots the mother ducks and their ducklings coming into view as they make their way around the island in Herbert Park's pond.

A frantic mother duck attacks the hunting heron. The mallard mothers' attacks are savage and the heron usually suffers a few bites and loses a feather or two, plucked from its body by the snapping mallards. The heron tries to avoid confrontations like this as much as possible. Airborne and shrieking loudly, today the heron avoids a nasty bite from this aggressive mallard.

The Heron Attacks

In a desperate attempt to flee the enormous predator, a tufted duck chick dives into the water.

But this experienced fish hunter has lightning fast reflexes. Stabbing the water, the heron submerges its head and grabs the chick between its beak. All the waterfowl are frantic by now and quacking loudly. The unfortunate chick's terrified chirping, however, can be heard above their loud vocals. Seconds later it is silenced – in one gulp the heron swallows the tiny duckling, whole and alive.

The ruthlessly efficient heron strikes again ... and again. The ducks' defences do slow the heron's, and the gulls', attacks down, however, and it's enough to see a percentage of their offspring survive and reach maturity.

Every year the tufted ducks return to the pond in Herbert Park to breed, staying until their chicks have matured, and every year they come face to face with the herons and the gulls.

This time the mother ducks were unable to prevent one of their offspring from being caught by the grey heron. The violent attacks from the mallards only served to slow the heron down. Although the tufted duckling dived beneath the water, it never had the speed to escape this experienced hunter.

Another unfortunate tufted duckling falls prey to the grey heron.

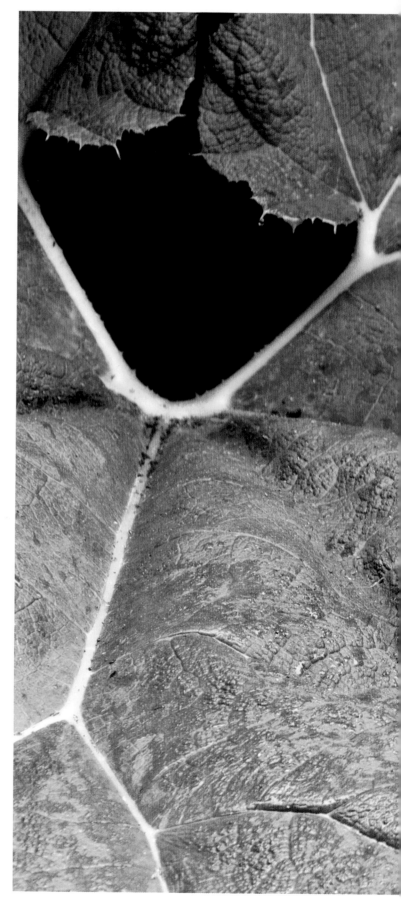

Tufted ducks are divers and like to find
their food – aquatic insects, molluscs
and some vegetation – beneath the
water. They dabble too, but diving and
underwater swimming is their
speciality, which prove an essential
adaptation when they are pursued by
predators at a young, flightless age.

From a brood of nine, only two tufted
ducklings remain. The grey heron and the
lesser black-backed gull have taken the rest.
The giant leaves of the Gunnera Tinctoria,
commonly known as giant rhubarb, have
become a favorite resting spot for the tufted
ducklings. This plant isn't native to Ireland,
but originates from South America.

Ducklings kill and eat insects throughout the day as part of their diet. When I see a duckling chase and snap at a beautiful butterfly floating above its head, I instinctively root for the butterfly and hope it gets away. Unfortunately, when an animal is designed to eat meat in order to survive, another must die. I trust in nature's wisdom and I have learned to accept its ways.

But no matter how many times I see a duckling caught and eaten by a predator, it always makes my heart sink and fills me with sadness. I can only hope that death is quick and that the ducklings don't experience too much trauma and pain. Scenes such as this show that nature's way is often brutal and merciless.

It is a real joy to watch the tufted ducklings diving and swimming under the water – their diving practice starts from their very first day on the water. And every so often their skills allow them to escape the heron's attacks by swimming out of sight. But sadly, more often than not, they are caught. Ducklings not only get attacked from the air, but also from the water. Many anglers have told me that they have seen pike (a large freshwater predatory fish) snatch a duckling or two as they paddle on the water. Some claim they have seen large trout do the same thing. Otters, mink and seals are other aquatic predators the ducklings need to avoid.

Ireland's Exotic Bird

You hear the kingfisher let out a loud high-pitched tweet, then you catch a glimpse of its exotic blue and aqua feathers zooming by at high speed. It will land at its favourite diving perch, from where it hunts the minnows that gather together in large numbers in the shallows at the river's edge.

The one thing I never tire of seeing is the kingfisher diving from a high branch headfirst into the river at high speed and catching a fish. Sometimes it spears the fish with its long sharp beak; other times it simply grasps the fish between its beak and resurfaces. Whenever the kingfisher catches a fish, it always immobilises it first by bashing it on a branch. Then the bird repositions the fish in its beak, making sure that it is swallowing the fish head first in order to prevent the scales from getting lodged in its throat.

In a flash of blue, the kingfisher zooms up and down the river – even a fleeting glimpse of it is enough to lift my day.

Minnows, each up to 3 inches long, gather in the shallows. Both the kingfisher and the heron like to prey on these tiny fish, catching many throughout the day.

Female kingfishers, like the one seen here, have a streak of orange under their lower bill, whereas the male's beak is all black. This particular species of kingfisher is known as the Eurasian Kingfisher, the River Kingfisher and the Common Kingfisher. I hate to use the word common when describing an animal as I feel it somehow devalues it – the kingfisher seen here is not at all common and is, in fact, a protected species.

Herbert Park's Special Guest

I spotted a yellow-bellied slider turtle in Herbert Park in the summer of 2008 and amazingly it was there again in the summer of 2009 – it had survived the Irish winter. It is normally found in the swamps of the southern states of the USA but can be bought as a pet here.

I have been told that people buy the turtles when they are very small and release them into park ponds and rivers when they have grown tired of taking care of them. The turtles use mud to cover themselves, which insulates and protects them from the winter's chill. Unfortunately these turtles pose a threat to the river's indigenous species.

There have been a few reports of such turtles being spotted on the River Dodder but only one on this stretch of the river – it was seen by a local angler, swimming around just below the foxes' den, then disappearing under the foliage on the bank.

This giant rhubarb leaf has become a great spot for basking in the sun.

Breakfast

Somehow half a dozen eggs, sausages and black and white pudding, all still in their wrappers, have wound up in the river.

The young heron leaves the eggs alone, but gulps down the sausages and pudding. I was a bit concerned about the heron's health because the pudding was still wrapped in plastic and tied at the end with a metal band. Thankfully, however, the young bird had no problems with its health and is still actively hunting along the river.

The heron swallows the still-wrapped black pudding in one gulp. And the white pudding goes the same way.

Worried Mother

A small piece of wood has found its way on to the pond in Herbert Park and the tiny tufted ducklings have found a use for it.

Sitting on their floating wooden island, the young chicks rest and preen their feathers. They have begun to drift from their mother's side and are now easier targets for the lesser black-backed gull that has already been busy hunting this year's chicks.

The mother calls out to her chicks, summoning them to her side, but the chicks take no notice and continue to drift around the pond. Not happy with this, their mother takes a more drastic form of action and tips the piece of wood over, dumping the surprised chicks into the water.

Her plan works and the chicks make their way back into her protective care.

The carefree tufted ducklings float around the pond, completely unaware of how vulnerable they are to an attack from the lesser black-backed gull that has been efficiently picking off mallard and tufted duck chicks that have strayed from their mothers' side.

The ducklings' clever mother makes use of her beak and tips over the little raft. The chicks are forced to abandon ship.

Not all the chicks get the message – one decides to climb back aboard but its mother doesn't look too pleased. In the end, all the chicks rejoin their mother and the safety of her protection far away from their little floating raft.

Sadly, later that day, one of the chicks lost its life to a lesser black-backed gull. Once again the ducklings floated away from the mother's side and one of them drifted so far behind that its capture by the gull went unnoticed by its mother. The chick seen here is a mallard chick but this gull took several chicks that day, hunting and catching both tufted and mallard ducklings from dawn till dusk.

Riverweed

The summer sun has brought this plant to life once again, adding a lush and vibrant look to the river. The local anglers call it 'riverweed'.

The foxes are fascinated by the weed and have come down to inspect the carpeted rocks. They sniff it and prod it, but decide not to taste or eat it.

The weed will die off soon but will reappear again next year.

The young foxes all showed an interest in the riverweed, trying to decide whether it was edible or not, when it sprang into life during the hot summer days.

The heron repeatedly dips the woodmouse
in and out of the river until it is lubricated
enough to be swallowed easily.

Rodent Hunter

The young heron has been hanging around a particular spot on the riverbank, catching small fish like sticklebacks and minnows. Occasionally the heron likes to poke its head in the Himalayan balsam and the tall shrubbery at the river's edge. This behaviour indicates that its attention has been drawn to the rustling and scurrying of the rats and mice that inhabit the riverbank.

One day, as dusk approaches, while fishing on the river, the heron suddenly cocks its head to the side and quickly stalks into the undergrowth. Immediately the heron becomes excited and twists its head and neck into an s-shaped pattern, so that its neck has a snake-like appearance.

The neck begins rapidly and repeatedly to twist and turn like a snake crawling along the ground – it's a sure sign that the heron is getting ready to take aim and snatch its prey. Seconds later it lunges forward, stabbing its beak and long neck into the foliage. The unfortunate rodent victim, a woodmouse, lets out a high-pitched squeal as the heron pulls itself from the foliage with the mouse caught between its beak. The mouse struggles vigorously to break free from the heron's grasp ... and succeeds!

The woodmouse hits the ground running and races back into the foliage but the heron gives chase and, seconds later, the mouse is recaptured and swallowed whole and alive.

Woodmice are mostly nocturnal and it is a rare privilege to see one during the day.

Night Hunters

The young foxes are now experienced night hunters. Brown rats are one of their favourite prey and are regularly pursued.

Rats are very active in the twilight hours and into the night ... and so are the foxes. The rats are great swimmers and many have escaped from a pursuing fox via the river. Some nights, though, I have heard the foxes hunting in between the bramble thickets, followed by the loud high-pitched squeals of a rat punctuating an otherwise silent night – one of the young foxes had caught its prey.

One night, I observed one of the young foxes pick up the trail of a brown rat, which led it to the rat's burrow on the riverbank. The fox sniffed around the entrance of the burrow for a second or two and then began pounding on the roof of the burrow with its feet. It then leapt in front of the burrow's entrance, then back onto the roof to pound some more – repeating this over and over, the fox was evidently trying to draw the rat out. It seemed as if the fox were expecting the rat to come running to the surface of the burrow out of fear or curiosity as to what was happening to the outside of its home. The fox appeared to have done this before, probably successfully – a trick possibly taught by its parents.

Luckily for tonight's rat, it decided to stay hidden beneath the ground.

Hunting rats at dusk. Two young foxes observe their sibling climb up into the thick vegetation on the riverbank, a place full of rat holes and a favourite hunting ground.

As the young mallards feed, the mother duck remains vigilant for the ever-present dangers on this stretch of the river. The young mallards' flight wings are beginning to show but it will still be another month before they will have developed sufficiently to enable them to fly out of harm's way.

I have previously seen the heron swallow a duckling of this size, if not bigger, whole. But, for some reason, it was unable to consume this female mallard duckling. The heron spent more than an hour dipping the duckling in and out of the water, punctuated by many failed attempts at swallowing the unfortunate bird. Sadly the young bird died during the protracted ordeal.

The heron simply dropped the duckling and left, but nothing is wasted on the river, and minutes later a magpie appeared and dragged the carcass out of the shallow water and up onto the riverbank. It was quickly joined by several more magpies who quarrelled for the rights to the best portions of this unexpected meal.

Constant Vigilance

The young foxes are always around and can regularly be seen watching the ducks and their families from the water's edge. The bank is their domain but, as long as the ducks stay vigilant when they are on the banks, they remain hard to catch. But it is the heron the waterfowl, wisely, fear the most on this stretch of the river. It can catch its prey whether they are in, on, or under the water.

Some of the mother ducks manage to protect their chicks from the predators long enough to see them develop their wings and fly out of harm's way. But until the young birds can fly, they are still very vulnerable to attack and capture.

This mother mallard has done well to have four of her chicks survive this far into their development – but she has lost two-thirds of her original brood to this hostile environment and will lose one more before her chicks fledge, a month from now. As they feed, she watches the riverbank closely – she and her young are dangerously close to the foxes' den.

The heron has not stopped preying on the large, flightless tufted ducklings either.

The Great Escape

As big as the young birds are now, the heron still manages to catch and swallow its unfortunate victims whole, although it can easily spend between fifteen minutes and an hour, sometimes even longer, trying to swallow the young ducks.

But at this size, the young ducks are much stronger. In the following series of photographs, the heron has plucked a flightless mallard drake from the pond in Herbert Park and flown up high into a tree. The heron's grip on the duckling wasn't great, however, and the struggling duckling managed to break free, plummeting 50 feet down. Luckily it hit the water, not the ground and, incredibly, remained unharmed.

The heron looked very surprised and fixed its eyes on the water below. The duckling wisely stayed under the water and swam for at least 30 feet before resurfacing out of the heron's line of sight. The duckling simply rejoined its mother and siblings and behaved as if nothing had happened.

The heron must not have been very hungry after all, as it did not bother looking any further for the duckling. Instead it remained in the tree and turned its attention to preening its feathers.

The heron soars up and over the pond
with the weighty duckling in its beak.

The heron stops on its favorite perch
in its favorite tree overlooking the
pond. Some light rain begins to fall.

The heron wants to manoeuvre the duckling
into a position where it can swallow it headfirst.
But the struggling young duck makes it hard
for the heron to keep its balance and maintain
a strong grip on its prey. Twisting and turning
the duckling manages to break free.

Hot Summer Days

The young foxes spend a lot of time down at the old river wall, just a short distance east of Ball's Bridge on the north side of the river. It's a favourite foraging spot for all the resident foxes.

The wall is crawling with insects and the young foxes can enjoy an easy meal – it's not much, but everything counts.

These two young foxes have discovered a suntrap by the wall and like to lounge around soaking up the heat from the hot rays.

This lucky young fox has spotted some woodlice crawling over the wall and simply picks them off one by one.

The young foxes are healthy and energetic and look stunning in their thickening ginger coats.

What a Fright!

Careful not to startle any fish, the grey heron moves slowly and precisely down the river.

Meanwhile, 600 feet upriver from the den, two young foxes fall asleep with the soft sound of the river flowing by.

Deeply focused on the job at hand, the hunting heron is completely unaware of the proximity of the two young predators. Suddenly the heron realises its precarious situation – shrieking loudly, the startled bird takes to the air.

One of the foxes wakes, lifts its sleepy head and stares at the screaming heron flying by. The heron lands 150 feet away and the young fox goes back to sleep.

The two young foxes can be seen sleeping, one at the bottom and one at the top of the riverbank. The heron is completely oblivious to their proximity.

The heron is hunting an aquatic creature – but not for long.

Screaming, the terrified heron flies away from the sleeping foxes. Its loud shrieks wake one of the foxes but, unbothered by all the commotion, it once again drops its sleepy head and goes back to sleep.

Breaking the Bond

Summer is coming to an end and the young foxes will soon be going their separate ways and leaving their parents' territory.

One evening I watched the vixen chasing her young down the riverbank. The young foxes didn't get the message and came back, making their way along the river's edge towards the den. The vixen spotted them and chased them again, even further downriver this time and under the railway bridge. She managed to catch up with one of them and gave it a few sharp bites before retreating back upriver. The young fox was not seriously hurt but it could be heard crying for a good hour beneath a bush.

It was a sad moment and I felt that the young fox was emotionally affected by its mother's unwelcoming behaviour, so different from her usual affectionate welcome. But now her intentions were to drive them away from her territory.

Sometimes the vixen keeps one of the females with her to help out with next year's litter, but I haven't seen it happen yet on this stretch of the river. The dog fox has always been around to help out, and is known to take over the vixen's role if anything were to happen to the vixen while she's raising her cubs.

Although the young foxes were strongly attached to their mother, they eventually left and were nowhere to be seen by the time spring arrived the following year.

This young fox is nearly five months old now, but will not reach its adult size for another couple of months. By the time they are nine to ten months old, some females have already reached sexual maturity.

Autumn Returns

It's once again time for the fish to take on the weirs and waterfalls in their monumental efforts to reach their spawning grounds.

Everywhere on the river the cycle of life continues.

The horse chestnut tree's nuts are falling to the ground and they litter the pavements that run alongside the river. The grey squirrels can be seen gathering up these nuts. This busy squirrel sits on top of the handrail that runs the length of the pedestrian bridge across the river by the railway station, with a chestnut in its mouth. The squirrels often use this handrail to cross the river.

EQUIPMENT AND TECHNIQUE

Here is a list of the equipment I used for the photographs for *Doorstep Wilderness*:

Canon EOS 7D

Canon PowerShot S410 (used once for the bee and flower photograph on page 176)

Canon EF 400 mm f/5.6L Telephoto Lens

Canon EF 70–300 mm f/4–5.6L IS (Image Stabiliser) USM Zoom Lens

Canon EF 24–105 mm f/4L IS USM (Ultrasonic Motor) Zoom Lens

Canon EF 70–200 mm f/4.5L USM Zoom Lens

Canon EF 100–400 mm f/4.5–5.6 IS USM Zoom Lens (rarely used)

Canon EF 2xII Extender

Canon RS–80N3 Remote Switch

Manfrotto monopod, Manfrotto tripod and a Joby GorillaPod

Bean bag, camouflage net and knee and back supports for carrying all the heavy equipment

Canon Mini DV Camcorder and Samsung Mini DV Camcorder

USING THE EQUIPMENT

To get the best photographs, a tremendous amount of time and energy is needed, so I like to be out working from 'sun up' to 'sun down' throughout the year.

During the summer months, I usually start the day at about 5.30 a.m. I have a good breakfast and pack my camera bag with plenty of water and fruit, and sometimes home-made sandwiches, before leaving for the first train that will take me to the river. I usually arrive at Lansdowne Road train station at about 6.30 a.m. and walk for two minutes down to where the foxes live on the riverbank.

I take my camera out of my camera bag and attach the remote switch cable to it. Then I set my bean bag down on the wall where I will eventually rest my camera. I manually set the exposure for the available light at the time. I usually set the aperture at 7.1 and adjust the shutter speed and ISO around this. The light changes regularly throughout the day – when light levels are low, the aperture is wide open on my 400 mm lens at 5.6, and the shutter speed and ISO are once again adjusted for exposure.

I always use a large bean bag weighing about 3 lb, and it is an excellent replacement for a tripod. I can place the bag on any object and then rest the camera on it; this allows me to take photos at very low shutter speeds and still get great results. To do this, I attach a remote switch cable to the camera and, keeping my body and hands as still as possible, I can carefully press the switch whenever I want. The camera never moves and the images are captured without blur. I only ever hold the camera by hand when I cannot use a tripod or a bean bag, or for action shots. To shoot these photos I have to increase the shutter speed to compensate for camera shake. I mainly use my 400 mm telephoto lens and, at the very least, I double the shutter speed based on the focal length (i.e. 800th of a second). If I have a lot of light, I will set the shutter speed as high as I can – this guarantees me a very sharp image.

My position on the riverbank allows me to capture all sorts of life stories. City debris often washes up on the bank after flooding from heavy rain. These items become perches for birds or playthings for young foxes – a shopping trolley becomes a favourite hang out for almost all of the river's residents. Perched in a pool of light on top of the trolley, a little robin is spotted by one of the cubs. Seeing an opportunity for a quick meal, the cub wastes no time and makes a dash towards the robin. At the very last minute, the robin escapes.

My only light source is the sun, the intensity of which changes throughout the day, depending on its position in the sky and the amount of cloud cover – all of which affects the amount of light reaching and illuminating the subject. So I constantly have to set and reset the camera to get a good exposure. I always set the camera manually and the metering is TTL (through the lens). If it were practical, I would use a light meter for quicker and more accurate results, but I know my equipment very well and can anticipate its response while metering the available light.

The photos, shot as RAW files, retain all the information that the camera captured at the time of shooting. Shooting RAW files allows me to correct images if they are slightly over- or underexposed. For practical reasons, I set the white balance to Auto, although it is usually a bit cooler than the light at the time of shooting. But I simply adjust this using Adobe Bridge RAW Converter to return it back to what I saw while shooting.

Once home, after I have uploaded the files to my computer, I back up the files on to two external hard drives. Then I take a look at the day's work and categorise and name each folder with the date and a brief description of the photographs. Later the files will be imported into Adobe Bridge Raw Converter in Photoshop CS4 – here the files are processed before I open them in Photoshop CS4, where I use levels and curves to adjust the contrast and brightness of the photos. I sharpen the photographs and save them as tiff files as sRGB or Adobe RGB colour profiles, depending on what use I have for them. I prefer to work in Standard Red Green and Blue, also known as sRGB. Although my computer monitor is good enough to work in Adobe RGB, the sRGB profile is the standard and this is compatible with all modern devices, so there is less of a chance of a colour mismatch.

The benefits of RAW are many. I usually correct the colour temperature and, if I have under- or overexposed the photos slightly, I can fix this in the Raw Converter.

I learn a lot from studying the photos on my computer. The camera cannot see as well as the human eye and the dynamic range is limited on my camera. I do not control the light when I shoot wildlife and I have only used a flash once for the photographs in this book – for the photo of the bee on the flower on page 176. So, if the light is difficult, I have to decide on what will be under- or overexposed.

RAW gives me great flexibility with the exposures and I can bring back details lost in tough lighting situations, especially on bright sunny days. Studying these results enables me to make better exposure decisions because I now know what details I will lose or save. With my experience of the riverbank and the available light throughout the day I have eventually beome quicker and better at photographing in difficult light.

I also film the wildlife using my EOS 7D in HD, and sometimes the mini DV camcorders I take with me, and upload some of these wildlife short videos to my YouTube channel. As with the photographs, I study this footage and this again helps me improve or imagine new photo ideas.

PRACTICALITIES

Although the animals are living in an urban area and are used to seeing people every day, they are still weary and easily scared. Loud bangs from car doors slamming shut or banging gates can startle the animals, especially the birds who immediately take flight. The sudden appearance of a person looking over the river wall will also have the same effect. It's never easy getting a photograph.

The river wall is perfect for concealing me from the wildlife's watchful eyes and also a great place for my camera to rest on my bean bag. I simply hunker down behind the wall, which hides my body, and the camera conceals my face. I also keep a camouflage net in my bag, which is great for throwing over the camera and me when I am in areas where I am not concealed too well.

I always wear dark clothing and, 90 per cent of the time, I wear black trousers and a jacket and a black shirt or jumper. Every now and then I will choose a brown or green jumper or shirt but I almost always prefer black. For a wildlife shoot you would normally wear traditional camouflage clothing but I had no need for that in this urban setting. I decided on black after observing the landscape – there are always dark patches in the foliage or dark shadows, so my dark clothing blends in well. I also noticed that the foxes and the heron did not pay attention to me standing by the river wall dressed in black, but they did take notice of anyone wearing a bright shirt or jumper.

I also wear a black baseball cap to keep the sun out of my eyes. I always wear boots that support my ankles – carrying all that heavy equipment over rocky or uneven terrain can cause a misstep and my sturdy boots have helped me avoid a twisted ankle many times. Waterproof boots are best for traversing through wet grass or standing in heavy rain – avoiding wet feet is a priority, especially on cold winter days.

The weather does not bother me – rain, sleet or snow. But the camera needs to stay dry. I made a waterproof cover from a green rain jacket I had and attached it to the lens hood using black masking tape. This is also an effective camouflage for the camera and lens. I love photographing wildlife in rough weather – it brings out the best in me and makes me feel more connected to the environment.

I always try to absorb the sounds made by the wildlife and the flowing river. Not only does this draw me in to the environment, it also clears my head of any distracting thoughts not related to my photography and the job at hand, and allows me to focus all my mental energy on capturing the desired images. I would recommend this to anyone who wants to relax their mind, especially listening to the sound of the steady flow of water as it passes over the river's rocks and boulders.

Although the river wall is a great help, it's not a perfect set up. Things happen very quickly when photographing wildlife – the animals are always moving around from one spot to another, never staying still for long. So getting the camera set up and ready, setting the exposure, etc, has to be done very quickly and correctly and the positioning the wall allows me is limited. Getting a good photo of the foxes drinking at the river's edge was very difficult and frustrating – the foxes were usually there and gone in ten to twenty seconds and getting the camera set up, lining up the shot, setting the exposure and then focusing on the fox was never easy, and it was a long time before I got the photos I wanted. The wall also vibrates slightly when a train passes over the Lansdowne Road railway bridge. So I would have to wait for the train to pass – because I was photographing in very low light and with very low shutter speeds (as low as one 30th of a second), the vibrations in the wall were enough to reduce the sharpness of the photograph. Many great opportunities were lost because of this or strong winds pushing against the camera and the lens.

Throughout the day I walk up and down the river, from Herbert Park down as far as London Bridge at Irishtown. But I spend the most amount of time between Ball's Bridge and the Lansdowne Road railway bridge. I observe and study the wildlife's behaviour at length – this is the only way to get to know the animals. The videos I shoot are a great help as I can spend more time at home studying the animals and the landscape in the videos.

STAYING MOTIVATED

The days are very long and an opportunity for a photo can arrive at any time – the worst thing that can happen is not being ready for the opportunity and subsequently messing up the shot. So I always try to be as fit and as well-fed as I can. Consequently, after arriving home and uploading the photos to my computer and external hard drives, I usually go straight to bed.

Being tired, cold and under-fed affect my mood and concentration – being relaxed and comfortable always produces successful decisions and photos. But most of the time I am very tired and hungry and cold and I just have to accept this and wait for the photo opportunity anyway. My strong desire to photograph a particular event on the river, such as the vixen nursing her young or the fish leaping up the cascading waters, give me energy and focus and motivate me through the long hard days.

Some of the photos I've included here have been published in all of our well-known Irish newspapers. They've also appeared in magazines and newspapers in the UK and throughout Europe and Asia, the USA and Canada, and published in books both here and abroad. Knowing that the images I take will reach a wide audience helps me stay energised and motivated – it is very rewarding to know that all my hard work is being seen and appreciated.